SIXTY POEMS

BY
RUDYARD KIPLING

SOME BLACK JACKET BOOKS

RUDYARD KIPLING

SIXTY POEMS

HODDER AND STOUGHTON
ST. PAUL'S HOUSE, LONDON, E.C.4

THIS EDITION FIRST PRINTED JULY 1939
REPRINTED . . . . . NOVEMBER 1939
REPRINTED . . . . . JUNE   1940
REPRINTED . . . . . NOVEMBER 1940
REPRINTED . . . . . DECEMBER 1940
REPRINTED . . . . . JUNE   1941
REPRINTED . . . . . JANUARY 1942
REPRINTED . . . . . NOVEMBER 1942
REPRINTED . . . . . MAY   1944
REPRINTED . . . . . DECEMBER 1945

Made and Printed in Great Britain for Hodder & Stoughton Limited,
by Wyman & Sons Limited, London, Reading and Fakenham

CONTENTS

DEDICATORY POEMS

CONTENTS

vi

CONTENTS

CONTENTS

CONTENTS

CONTENTS

DEDICATORY POEMS

THE FIRES

(Prelude to Collected Verse)

MEN make them fires on the hearth
    Each under his roof-tree,
And the Four Winds that rule the earth
    They blow the smoke to me.

Across the high hills and the sea
    And all the changeful skies,
The Four Winds blow the smoke to me
    Till the tears are in my eyes.

Until the tears are in my eyes
    And my heart is wellnigh broke
For thinking on old memories
    That gather in the smoke.

With every shift of every wind
    The homesick memories come,
From every quarter of mankind
    Where I have made me a home.

Four times a fire against the cold
    And a roof against the rain—
Sorrow fourfold and joy fourfold
    The Four Winds bring again !

How can I answer which is best
    Of all the fires that burn?
I have been too often host or guest
    At every fire in turn.

How can I turn from any fire,
    On any man's hearthstone?
I know the wonder and desire
    That went to build my own!

How can I doubt man's joy or woe
    Where'er his house-fires shine,
Since all that man must undergo
    Will visit me at mine?

Oh, you Four Winds that blow so strong
    And know that this is true,
Stoop for a little and carry my song
    To all the men I knew!

Where there are fires against the cold,
    Or roofs against the rain—
With love fourfold and joy fourfold,
    Take them my songs again!

DEDICATION FROM "BARRACK-ROOM BALLADS"

BEYOND the path of the outmost sun through
    utter darkness hurled—
Farther than ever comet flared or vagrant star-
    dust swirled—
Live such as fought and sailed and ruled and
    loved and made our world.

They are purged of pride because they died;
    they know the worth of their bays;
They sit at wine with the Maidens Nine and the
    Gods of the Elder Days—
It is their will to serve or be still as fitteth Our
    Father's praise.

'Tis theirs to sweep through the ringing deep
    where Azrael's outposts are,
Or buffet a path through the Pit's red wrath when
    God goes out to war,
Or hang with the reckless Seraphim on the rein
    of a red-maned star.

They take their mirth in the joy of the Earth—
    they dare not grieve for her pain.
They know of toil and the end of toil; they know
    God's Law is plain;
So they whistle the Devil to make them sport
    who know that Sin is vain.

And oft-times cometh our wise Lord God, master
    of every trade,

5

And tells them tales of His daily toil, of Edens
    newly made ;
And they rise to their feet as He passes by,
    gentlemen unafraid.

To these who are cleansed of base Desire, Sorrow
    and Lust and Shame—
Gods for they knew the hearts of men, men for
    they stooped to Fame—
Borne on the breath that men call Death, my
    brother's spirit came.

He scarce had need to doff his pride or slough
    the dross of Earth—
E'en as he trod that day to God so walked he
    from his birth,
In simpleness and gentleness and honour and
    clean mirth.

So cup to lip in fellowship they gave him welcome
    high
And made him place at the banquet board—the
    Strong Men ranged thereby,
Who had done his work and held his peace and
    had no fear to die.

Beyond the loom of the last lone star, through open
    darkness hurled,
Further than rebel comet dared or hiving star-
    swarm swirled,
Sits he with those that praise our God for that they
    served His world.

"MY NEW-CUT ASHLAR"

My NEW-CUT ashlar takes the light
Where crimson-blank the windows flare.
By my own work before the night,
Great Overseer, I make my prayer.

If there be good in that I wrought
Thy Hand compelled it, Master, Thine—
Where I have failed to meet Thy Thought
I know, through Thee, the blame was mine.

One instant's toil to Thee denied
Stands all Eternity's offence.
Of that I did with Thee to guide,
To Thee, through Thee, be excellence.

The depth and dream of my desire,
The bitter paths wherein I stray—
Thou knowest Who hast made the Fire,
Thou knowest Who hast made the Clay.

Who, lest all thought of Eden fade,
Bring'st Eden to the craftsman's brain—
Godlike to muse o'er his own Trade
And manlike stand with God again!

One stone the more swings into place
In that dread Temple of Thy worth.
It is enough that, through Thy Grace,
I saw nought common on Thy Earth.

Take not that vision from my ken—
Oh whatsoe'er may spoil or speed.
Help me to need no aid from men
That I may help such men as need !

L'ENVOI

(*Departmental Ditties*)

THE smoke upon your Altar dies,
    The flowers decay,
The Goddess of your sacrifice
    Has flown away.
What profit then to sing or slay
The sacrifice from day to day ?

" We know the Shrine is void," they said,
    " The Goddess flown—
" Yet wreaths are on the altar laid—
    " The Altar-Stone
" Is black with fumes of sacrifice,
" Albeit She has fled our eyes.

" For, it may be, if still we sing
    " And tend the Shrine,
" Some Deity on wandering wing
    " May there incline ;
" And, finding all in order meet,
" Stay while we worship at Her feet."

ENGLAND AND EMPIRE

A SONG OF THE ENGLISH

1893

FAIR is our lot—O goodly is our heritage !
(Humble ye, my people, and be fearful in your mirth l)
  For the Lord our God Most High
  He hath made the deep as dry,
He hath smote for us a pathway to the ends of all the
    Earth !

Yea, though we sinned, and our rulers went from
    righteousness—
Deep in all dishonour though we stained our garments'
    hem,
  Oh be ye not dismayed,
  Though we stumbled and we strayed,
We were led by evil counsellors—the Lord shall deal
    with them !

Hold ye the Faith—the Faith our Fathers sealed us,
Whoring not with visions—overwise and overstale.
  Except ye pay the Lord
  Single heart and single sword,
Of your children in their bondage He shall ask them
    treble-tale !

Keep ye the Law—be swift in all obedience—
Clear the land of evil, drive the road and bridge the ford.

Make ye sure to each his own
That he reap where he hath sown ;
By the peace among Our peoples let men know we serve
the Lord !

.   .   .   .   .

Hear now a song—a song of broken interludes—
A song of little cunning ; of a singer nothing worth.
Through the naked words and mean
May ye see the truth between,
As the singer knew and touched it in the ends of all the
Earth !

THE COASTWISE LIGHTS

OUR brows are bound with spindrift and the weed
    is on our knees ;
Our loins are battered 'neath us by the swinging,
    smoking seas.
From reef and rock and skerry—over headland,
    ness, and voe—
The Coastwise Lights of England watch the ships
    of England go !

Through the endless summer evenings, on the
    lineless, level floors ;
Through the yelling Channel tempest when the
    siren hoots and roars—

By day the dipping house-flag and by night the
    rocket's trail—
As the sheep that graze behind us so we know
    them where they hail.

We bridge across the dark, and bid the helmsman
    have a care,
The flash that, wheeling inland, wakes his sleeping
    wife to prayer.
From our vexed eyries, head to gale, we bind in
    burning chains
The lover from the sea-rim drawn—his love in
    English lanes.

We greet the clippers wing-and-wing that race the
    Southern wool ;
We warn the crawling cargo-tanks of Bremen,
    Leith, and Hull ;
To each and all our equal lamp at peril of the sea—
The white wall-sided warships or the whalers of
    Dundee !

Come up, come in from Eastward, from the guard-
    ports of the Morn !
Beat up, beat in from Southerly, O gipsies of the
    Horn !

Swift shuttles of an Empire's loom that weave us
    main to main,
The Coastwise Lights of England give you welcome
    back again !

Go, get you gone up-Channel with the sea-crust
    on your plates ;
Go, get you into London with the burden of your
    freights !
Haste, for they talk of Empire there, and say, if
    any seek,
The Lights of England sent you and by silence
    shall ye speak !

THE SONG OF THE DEAD

*HEAR now the Song of the Dead—in the North by
    the torn berg-edges—
They that look still to the Pole, asleep by their hide-
    stripped sledges.
Song of the Dead in the South—in the sun by their
    skeleton horses,
Where the warrigal whimpers and bays through the dust
    of the sere river-courses.*

*Song of the Dead in the East—in the heat-rotted jungle-
    hollows,*

*Where the dog-ape barks in the kloof—in the brake of
    the buffalo-wallows.*
*Song of the Dead in the West—in the Barrens, the pass
    that betrayed them,*
*Where the wolverine tumbles their packs from the camp
    and the grave-mound they made them ;*
        Hear now the Song of the Dead !

I

We were dreamers, dreaming greatly, in the man-
    stifled town ;
We yearned beyond the sky-line where the strange
    roads go down.
Came the Whisper, came the Vision, came the
    Power with the Need,
Till the Soul that is not man's soul was lent us to
    lead.

As the deer breaks—as the steer breaks—from
    the herd where they graze,
In the faith of little children we went on our ways.
Then the wood failed—then the food failed—then
    the last water dried—
In the faith of little children we lay down and died.
On the sand-drift—on the veldt-side—in the fern-
    scrub we lay,

That our sons might follow after by the bones
    on the way.
Follow after—follow after! We have watered
    the root,
And the bud has come to blossom that ripens for
    fruit!
Follow after—we are waiting, by the trails that we
    lost,
For the sounds of many footsteps, for the tread of
    a host.
Follow after—follow after—for the harvest is
    sown :
By the bones about the wayside ye shall come to
    your own!

When Drake went down to the Horn
And England was crowned thereby,
'Twixt seas unsailed and shores unhailed
Our Lodge—our Lodge was born
(And England was crowned thereby!)

Which never shall close again
By day nor yet by night,
While man shall take his life to stake
At risk of shoal or main
(By day nor yet by night)

But standeth even so
  As now we witness here,
While men depart, of joyful heart,
  Adventure for to know
  (As now bear witness here !)

II

We have fed our sea for a thousand years
  And she calls us, still unfed,
Though there's never a wave of all her waves
  But marks our English dead :
We have strawed our best to the weed's unrest,
  To the shark and the sheering gull.
If blood be the price of admiralty,
  Lord God, we ha' paid in full !

There's never a flood goes shoreward now
  But lifts a keel we manned ;
There's never an ebb goes seaward now
  But drops our dead on the sand—
But slinks our dead on the sands forlore,
  From the Ducies to the Swin.
If blood be the price of admiralty,
If blood be the price of admiralty,
  Lord God, we ha' paid it in !

We must feed our sea for a thousand years,
    For that is our doom and pride,
As it was when they sailed with the *Golden Hind*,
    Or the wreck that struck last tide—
Or the wreck that lies on the spouting reef
    Where the ghastly blue-lights flare.
If blood be the price of admiralty,
If blood be the price of admiralty,
If blood be the price of admiralty,
    Lord God, we ha' bought it fair !

THE DEEP-SEA CABLES

THE wrecks dissolve above us ; their dust drops
    down from afar—
Down to the dark, to the utter dark, where the
    blind white sea-snakes are.
There is no sound, no echo of sound, in the deserts
    of the deep,
Or the great grey level plains of ooze where the
    shell-burred cables creep.

Here in the womb of the world—here on the tie-
    ribs of earth
    Words, and the words of men, flicker and flutter
    and beat—
Warning, sorrow, and gain, salutation and mirth—
    For a Power troubles the Still that has neither
    voice nor feet.

They have wakened the timeless Things; they
    have killed their father Time;
  Joining hands in the gloom, a league from the
    last of the sun.
Hush! Men talk to-day o'er the waste of the
    ultimate slime,
  And a new Word runs between: whispering,
    "Let us be one!"

THE SONG OF THE SONS

ONE from the ends of the earth—gifts at an open
    door—
Treason has much, but we, Mother, thy sons have
    more!
From the whine of a dying man, from the snarl
    of a wolf-pack freed,
Turn, and the world is thine. Mother, be proud
    of thy seed!
Count, are we feeble or few? Hear, is our speech
    so rude?
Look, are we poor in the land? Judge, are we
    men of The Blood?

Those that have stayed at thy knees, Mother, go
    call them in—
We that were bred overseas wait and would speak
    with our kin.

Not in the dark do we fight—haggle and flout and
    gibe ;
Selling our love for a price, loaning our hearts for a
    bribe.
Gifts have we only to-day—Love without promise
    or fee—
Hear, for thy children speak, from the uttermost
    parts of the sea !

THE SONG OF THE CITIES

BOMBAY

ROYAL and Dower-royal, I the Queen
    Fronting thy richest sea with richer hands—
A thousand mills roar through me where I glean
    All races from all lands.

CALCUTTA

Me the Sea-captain loved, the River built,
    Wealth sought and Kings adventured life to
      hold.
Hail, England ! I am Asia—Power on silt,
    Death in my hands, but Gold !

MADRAS

Clive kissed me on the mouth and eyes and brow,
    Wonderful kisses, so that I became
Crowned above Queens—a withered beldame now,
    Brooding on ancient fame.

RANGOON

Hail, Mother ! Do they call me rich in trade ?
    Little care I, but hear the shorn priest drone,
And watch my silk-clad lovers, man by maid,
    Laugh 'neath my Shwe Dagon.

SINGAPORE

Hail, Mother ! East and West must seek my aid
    Ere the spent hull may dare the ports afar.
The second doorway of the wide world's trade
    Is mine to loose or bar.

HONG-KONG

Hail, Mother ! Hold me fast ; my Praya sleeps
    Under innumerable keels to-day.
Yet guard (and landward), or to-morrow sweeps
    Thy warships down the bay !

HALIFAX

Into the mist my guardian prows put forth,
  Behind the mist my virgin ramparts lie,
The Warden of the Honour of the North,
  Sleepless and veiled am I !

QUEBEC AND MONTREAL

Peace is our portion.   Yet a whisper rose,
  Foolish and causeless, half in jest, half hate.
Now wake we and remember mighty blows,
  And, fearing no man, wait !

VICTORIA

From East to West the circling word has passed,
  Till West is East beside our land-locked blue ;
From East to West the tested chain holds fast,
  The well-forged link rings true !

CAPETOWN

Hail !   Snatched and bartered oft from hand to
      hand,
  I dream my dream, by rock and heath and pine,
Of Empire to the northward.   Ay, one land
  From Lion's Head to Line !

22

MELBOURNE

Greeting !   Nor fear nor favour won us place,
  Got between greed of gold and dread of drouth,
Loud-voiced and reckless as the wild tide-race
  That whips our harbour-mouth !

SYDNEY

Greeting !   My birth-stain have I turned to good ;
  Forcing strong wills perverse to steadfastness :
The first flush of the tropics in my blood,
  And at my feet Success !

BRISBANE

The northern stock beneath the southern skies—
  I build a Nation for an Empire's need,
Suffer a little, and my land shall rise,
  Queen over lands indeed !

HOBART

Man's love first found me ;   man's hate made me
      Hell ;
  For my babes' sake I cleansed those infamies.
Earnest for leave to live and labour well,
  God flung me peace and ease.

AUCKLAND

Last, loneliest, loveliest, exquisite, apart—
  On us, on us the unswerving season smiles,
Who wonder 'mid our fern why men depart
  To seek the Happy Isles !

ENGLAND'S ANSWER

TRULY ye come of The Blood ; slower to bless
    than to ban,
Little used to lie down at the bidding of any man—
Flesh of the flesh that I bred, bone of the bone that
    I bare ;
Stark as your sons shall be—stern as your fathers
    were.
Deeper than speech our love, stronger than life
    our tether,
But we do not fall on the neck nor kiss when we
    come together.
My arm is nothing weak, my strength is not gone
    by ;
Sons, I have borne many sons, but my dugs are
    not dry.
Look, I have made ye a place and opened wide the
    doors,
That ye may talk together, your Barons and
    Councillors—
Wards of the Outer March, Lords of the Lower
    Seas,

Ay, talk to your grey mother that bore you on her
knees !—

That ye may talk together, brother to brother's
face—

Thus for the good of your peoples—thus for the
Pride of the Race.

Also, we will make promise. So long as The
Blood endures,

I shall know that your good is mine : ye shall feel
that my strength is yours :

In the day of Armageddon, at the last great fight
of all,

That Our House stand together and the pillars do
not fall.

Draw now the threefold knot firm on the ninefold
bands,

And the Law that ye make shall be law after the
rule of your lands.

This for the waxen Heath, and that for the Wattle-
bloom,

This for the Maple-leaf, and that for the Southern
Broom.

The Law that ye make shall be law and I do not
press my will,

Because ye are Sons of The Blood and call me
Mother still.

Now must ye speak to your kinsmen and they must
speak to you,

After the use of the English, in straight-flung
words and few.

Go to your work and be strong, halting not in your
    ways,
Baulking the end half-won for an instant dole of
    praise.
Stand to your work and be wise—certain of sword
    and pen,
Who are neither children nor Gods, but men in a
    world of men !

THE RIVER'S TALE

(PREHISTORIC)

TWENTY bridges from Tower to Kew
Wanted to know what the River knew,
For they were young and the Thames was old,
And this is the tale that the River told :—

" I walk my beat before London Town,
Five hours up and seven down.
Up I go till I end my run
At Tide-end-town, which is Teddington.
Down I come with the mud in my hands
And plaster it over the Maplin Sands.
But I'd have you know that these waters of mine
Were once a branch of the River Rhine,

When hundreds of miles to the East I went
And England was joined to the Continent.

I remember the bat-winged lizard-birds,
The Age of Ice and the mammoth herds,
And the giant tigers that stalked them down
Through Regent's Park into Camden Town.
And I remember like yesterday
The earliest Cockney who came my way,
When he pushed through the forest that lined the
     Strand,
With paint on his face and a club in his hand.
He was death to feather and fin and fur.
He trapped my beavers at Westminster.
He netted my salmon, he hunted my deer,
He killed my heron off Lambeth Pier.
He fought his neighbour with axes and swords,
Flint or bronze, at my upper fords,
While down at Greenwich, for slaves and tin,
The tall Phoenician ships stole in,
And North Sea war-boats, painted and gay,
Flashed like dragon-flies, Erith way ;
And Norseman and Negro and Gaul and Greek
Drank with the Britons in Barking Creek,
And life was gay, and the world was new,
And I was a mile across at Kew !
But the Roman came with a heavy hand,
And bridged and roaded and ruled the land,
And the Roman left and the Danes blew in---
And that's where your history-books begin ! "

THE LAND

WHEN Julius Fabricius, Sub-Prefect of the Weald,
In the days of Diocletian owned our Lower River-
field,
He called to him Hobdenius—a Briton of the Clay,
Saying : " What about that River-piece for layin'
in to hay ? "

And the aged Hobden answered : " I remember
as a lad
My father told your father that she wanted dreenin'
bad.
An' the more that you neeglect her the less you'll
get her clean.
Have it jest *as* you've a mind to, but, if I was you,
I'd dreen."

So they drained it long and crossways in the lavish
Roman style—
Still we find among the river-drift their flakes of
ancient tile,
And in drouthy middle August, when the bones of
meadows show,
We can trace the lines they followed sixteen hundred
years ago.

Then Julius Fabricius died as even Prefects do,
And after certain centuries, Imperial Rome died
too.

And when the spates of Autumn whirl the gravel-
    beds away
You can see their faithful fragments, iron-hard in
    iron clay.

.   .   .   .   .

Georgii Quinti Anno Sexto, I, who own the River-
    field,
Am fortified with title-deeds, attested, signed and
    sealed,
Guaranteeing me, my assigns, my executors and
    heirs
All sorts of powers and profits which—are neither
    mine nor theirs.

I have rights of chase and warren, as my dignity
    requires.
I can fish—but Hobden tickles. I can shoot—
    but Hobden wires.
I repair, but he reopens, certain gaps which, men
    allege,
Have been used by every Hobden since a Hobden
    swapped a hedge.

Shall I dog his morning progress o'er the track-
    betraying dew ?
Demand his dinner-basket into which my pheasant
    flew ?
Confiscate his evening faggot under which my
    conies ran,
And summons him to judgment ?   I would sooner
    summons Pan.

His dead are in the churchyard—thirty generations laid.

Their names were old in history when Domesday Book was made ;

And the passion and the piety and prowess of his line

Have seeded, rooted, fruited in some land the Law calls mine.

Not for any beast that burrows, not for any bird that flies,

Would I lose his large sound council, miss his keen amending eyes.

He is bailiff, woodman, wheelwright, field-surveyor, engineer,

And if flagrantly a poacher—'tain't for me to interfere.

" Hob, what about that River-bit ? " I turn to him again,

With Fabricius and Ogier and William of Warenne.

" Hev it jest as you've a mind to, *but* "—and here he takes command.

For whoever pays the taxes old Mus' Hobden owns the land.

THE ROMAN CENTURION'S SONG

(ROMAN OCCUPATION OF BRITAIN, A.D. 300)

LEGATE, I had the news last night—my cohort
    ordered home
By ship to Portus Itius and thence by road to Rome.
I've marched the companies aboard, the arms are
    stowed below :
Now let another take my sword. Command me
    not to go !

I've served in Britain forty years, from Vectis to
    the Wall.
I have none other home than this, nor any life
    at all.
Last night I did not understand, but, now the hour
    draws near
That calls me to my native land, I feel that land is
    here.

Here where men say my name was made, here
    where my work was done ;
Here where my dearest dead are laid—my wife—
    my wife and son ;
Here where time, custom, grief and toil, age,
    memory, service, love,
Have rooted me in British soil. Ah, how can I
    remove ?

For me this land, that sea, these airs, those folk and
fields suffice.
What purple Southern pomp can match our
changeful Northern skies,
Black with December snows unshed or pearled
with August haze—
The clanging arch of steel-grey March, or June's
long-lighted days ?

You'll follow widening Rhodanus till vine and olive
lean
Aslant before the sunny breeze that sweeps
Nemausus clean
To Arelate's triple gate ; but let me linger on,
Here where our stiff-necked British oaks confront
Euroclydon !

You'll take the old Aurelian Road through shore-
descending pines
Where, blue as any peacock's neck, the Tyrrhene
Ocean shines.
You'll go where laurel crowns are won, but—will
you e'er forget
The scent of hawthorn in the sun, or bracken in
the wet ?

Let me work here for Britain's sake—at any task
you will—
A marsh to drain, a road to make or native troops
to drill.

rn camp (I know the Pict) or granite
keep,
heather derelict, where our old mess-
leep.

ne to you in tears—My cohort ordered

in Britain forty years.   What should I
Rome ?
heart, my soul, my mind—the only life

annot leave it all behind.   Command me not to
go !

THE WAY THROUGH THE WOODS

THEY shut the road through the woods
Seventy years ago.
Weather and rain have undone it again,
And now you would never know
There was once a road through the woods
Before they planted the trees.
It is underneath the coppice and heath,
And the thin anemones.
Only the keeper sees
That, where the ring-dove broods,
And the badgers roll at ease,
There was once a road through the woods.

Yet, if you enter the woods
Of a summer evening late,
When the night-air cools on the trout-ringed pools
Where the otter whistles his mate,
(They fear not men in the woods,
Because they see so few.)
You will hear the beat of a horse's feet,
And the swish of a skirt in the dew,
Steadily cantering through
The misty solitudes,
As though they perfectly knew
The old lost road through the woods. . . .
But there is no road through the woods.

A TREE SONG

(A.D. 1200)

OF ALL the trees that grow so fair,
  Old England to adorn,
Greater are none beneath the Sun,
  Than Oak, and Ash, and Thorn.
Sing Oak, and Ash, and Thorn, good sirs,
  (All of a Midsummer morn!)
Surely we sing no little thing,
  In Oak, and Ash, and Thorn!

Oak of the Clay lived many a day,
  Or ever Æneas began.
Ash of the Loam was a lady at home,
  When Brut was an outlaw man.

Thorn of the Down saw New Troy Town
  (From which was London born);
Witness hereby the ancientry
  Of Oak, and Ash, and Thorn!

Yew that is old in churchyard-mould,
  He breedeth a mighty bow.
Alder for shoes do wise men choose,
  And beech for cups also.
But when ye have killed, and your bowl is spilled,
  And your shoes are clean outworn,
Back ye must speed for all that ye need,
  To Oak, and Ash, and Thorn!

Ellum she hateth mankind, and waiteth
  Till every gust be laid,
To drop a limb on the head of him
  That anyway trusts her shade.
But whether a lad be sober or sad,
  Or mellow with ale from the horn,
He will take no wrong when he lieth along
  'Neath Oak, and Ash, and Thorn!

Oh, do not tell the Priest our plight,
  Or he would call it a sin;
But—we have been out in the woods all night,
  A-conjuring Summer in!
And we bring you news by word of mouth—
  Good news for cattle and corn—
Now is the Sun come up from the South,
  With Oak, and Ash, and Thorn!

Sing Oak, and Ash, and Thorn, good sirs
  (All of a Midsummer morn) !
England shall bide till Judgment Tide,
  By Oak, and Ash, and Thorn !

THE GLORY OF THE GARDEN

OUR England is a garden that is full of stately
    views,
Of borders, beds and shrubberies and lawns and
    avenues,
With statues on the terraces and peacocks strutting
    by ;
But the Glory of the Garden lies in more than
    meets the eye.

For where the old thick laurels grow, along the
    thin red wall,
You find the tool- and potting-sheds which are the
    heart of all ;
The cold-frames and the hot-houses, the dungpits
    and the tanks,
The rollers, carts and drain-pipes, with the barrows
    and the planks.

And there you'll see the gardeners, the men and
    'prentice boys
Told off to do as they are bid and do it without
    noise ;
For, except when seeds are planted and we shout
    to scare the birds,
The Glory of the Garden it abideth not in words.

And some can pot begonias and some can bud a
    rose,
And some are hardly fit to trust with anything that
    grows ;
But they can roll and trim the lawns and sift the
    sand and loam,
For the Glory of the Garden occupieth all who
    come.

Our England is a garden, and such gardens are
    not made
By singing :—" Oh, how beautiful ! " and sitting
    in the shade,
While better men than we go out and start their
    working lives
At grubbing weeds from gravel-paths with broken
    dinner-knives.

There's not a pair of legs so thin, there's not a
    head so thick,
There's not a hand so weak and white, nor yet a
    heart so sick,
But it can find some needful job that's crying to
    be done,
For the Glory of the Garden glorifieth every one.

Then seek your job with thankfulness and work
    till further orders,
If it's only netting strawberries or killing slugs on
    borders ;

And when your back stops aching and your hands
  begin to harden,
You will find yourself a partner in the Glory of
  the Garden.

Oh, Adam was a gardener, and God who made
  him sees
That half a proper gardener's work is done upon
  his knees,
So when your work is finished, you can wash your
  hands and pray
For the Glory of the Garden, that it may not pass
  away !
And the Glory of the Garden it shall never pass away !

SUSSEX

1902

God gave all men all earth to love,
  But since our hearts are small,
Ordained for each one spot should prove
  Belovèd over all ;
That, as He watched Creation's birth,
  So we, in godlike mood,
May of our love create our earth
  And see that it is good.

So one shall Baltic pines content,
　　As one some Surrey glade,
Or one the palm-grove's droned lament
　　Before Levuka's Trade.
Each to his choice, and I rejoice
　　The lot has fallen to me
In a fair ground—in a fair ground—
　　Yea, Sussex by the sea !

No tender-hearted garden crowns,
　　No bosomed woods adorn
Our blunt, bow-headed, whale-backed Downs,
　　But gnarled and writhen thorn—
Bare slopes where chasing shadows skim,
　　And, through the gaps revealed,
Belt upon belt, the wooded, dim,
　　Blue goodness of the Weald.

Clean of officious fence or hedge,
　　Half-wild and wholly tame,
The wise turf cloaks the white cliff edge
　　As when the Romans came.
What sign of those that fought and died
　　At shift of sword and sword ?
The barrow and the camp abide,
　　The sunlight and the sward.

Here leaps ashore the full Sou'west
　　All heavy-winged with brine,
Here lies above the folded crest
　　The Channel's leaden line ;

And here the sea-fogs lap and cling,
    And here, each warning each,
The sheep-bells and the ship-bells ring
    Along the hidden beach.

We have no waters to delight
    Our broad and brookless vales—
Only the dewpond on the height
    Unfed, that never fails—
Whereby no tattered herbage tells
    Which way the season flies—
Only our close-bit thyme that smells
    Like dawn in Paradise.

Here, through the strong and shadeless days
    The tinkling silence thrills ;
Or little, lost, Down churches praise
    The Lord who made the hills :
But here the Old Gods guard their round,
    And, in her secret heart,
The heathen kingdom Wilfrid found
    Dreams, as she dwells, apart.

Though all the rest were all my share,
    With equal soul I'd see
Her nine-and-thirty sisters fair,
    Yet none more fair than she.
Choose ye your need from Thames to Tweed,
    And I will choose instead
Such lands as lie 'twixt Rake and Rye,
    Black Down and Beachy Head.

I will go out against the sun
    Where the rolled scarp retires,

And the Long Man of Wilmington
   Looks naked toward the shires ;
And east till doubling Rother crawls
   To find the fickle tide,
By dry and sea-forgotten walls,
   Our ports of stranded pride.

I will go north about the shaws
   And the deep ghylls that breed
Huge oaks and old, the which we hold
   No more than Sussex weed ;
Or south where windy Piddinghoe's
   Begilded dolphin veers
And red beside wide-bankèd Ouse
   Lie down our Sussex steers.

So to the land our hearts we give
   Till the sure magic strike,
And Memory, Use, and Love make live
   Us and our fields alike—
That deeper than our speech and thought,
   Beyond our reason's sway,
Clay of the pit whence we were wrought
   Yearns to its fellow-clay.

God gives all men all earth to love,
   But since man's heart is small,
Ordains for each one spot shall prove
   Belovèd over all.
Each to his choice, and I rejoice
   The lot has fallen to me
In a fair ground—in a fair ground—
   Yea, Sussex by the sea !

A SCHOOL SONG

(Prelude to Stalky and Co.)

" *LET us now praise famous men* "—
  Men of little showing—
For their work continueth,
And their work continueth,
Broad and deep continueth,
  Greater than their knowing!

Western wind and open surge
  Took us from our mothers—
Flung us on a naked shore
(Twelve bleak houses by the shore!
Seven summers by the shore!)
  'Mid two hundred brothers.

There we met with famous men
  Set in office o'er us;
And they beat on us with rods—
Faithfully with many rods—
Daily beat us on with rods,
  For the love they bore us!

Out of Egypt unto Troy—
  Over Himalaya—
Far and sure our bands have gone—
Hy-Brazil or Babylon,
Islands of the Southern Run,
  And Cities of Cathaia!

And we all praise famous men—
  Ancients of the College;

For they taught us common sense—
Tried to teach us common sense—
Truth and God's Own Common Sense,
    Which is more than knowledge !

Each degree of Latitude
    Strung about Creation
Seeth one or more of us
(Of one muster each of us),
Diligent in that he does,
    Keen in his vocation.

This we learned from famous men,
    Knowing not its uses,
When they showed, in daily work,
Man must finish off his work—
Right or wrong, his daily work—
    And without excuses.

Servants of the Staff and chain,
    Mine and fuse and grapnel—
Some, before the face of Kings,
Stand before the face of Kings ;
Bearing gifts to divers Kings—
    Gifts of case and shrapnel.

This we learned from famous men
    Teaching in our borders,
Who declarèd it was best,
Safest, easiest, and best—
Expeditious, wise, and best—
    To obey your orders.

Some beneath the further stars
  Bear the greater burden :
Set to serve the lands they rule,
(Save he serve no man may rule),
Serve and love the lands they rule ;
  Seeking praise nor guerdon.

This we learned from famous men,
  Knowing not we learned it.
Only, as the years went by—
Lonely, as the years went by—
Far from help as years went by,
  Plainer we discerned it.

Wherefore praise we famous men
  From whose bays we borrow—
They that put aside To-day—
All the joys of their To-day—
And with toil of their To-day
  Bought for us To-morrow !

Bless and praise we famous men—
  Men of little showing—
For their work continueth,
And their work continueth,
Broad and deep continueth,
  Great beyond their knowing !

TOMMY

I WENT into a public-'ouse to get a pint o' beer,
The publican 'e up an' sez, "We serve no red-
    coats here."

The girls be'ind the bar they laughed an' giggled
    fit to die,
I outs into the street again an' to myself sez I :
    O it's Tommy this, an' Tommy that, an'
        " Tommy, go away " ;
    But it's " Thank you, Mister Atkins," when
        the band begins to play—
    The band begins to play, my boys, the band
        begins to play,
    O it's " Thank you, Mister Atkins," when the
        band begins to play.

I went into a theatre as sober as could be,
They gave a drunk civilian room, but 'adn't none
    for me ;
They sent me to the gallery or round the music-'alls,
But when it comes to fightin', Lord ! they'll shove
    me in the stalls !
    For it's Tommy this, an' Tommy that, an'
        " Tommy, wait outside " ;
    But it's " Special train for Atkins " when the
        trooper's on the tide—
    The troopship's on the tide, my boys, the
        troopship's on the tide,
    O it's " Special train for Atkins " when the
        trooper's on the tide.

Yes, makin' mock o' uniforms that guard you
    while you sleep
Is cheaper than them uniforms, an' they're star-
    vation cheap ;

An' hustlin' drunken soldiers when they're goin'
    large a bit
Is five times better business than paradin' in full kit.
    Then it's Tommy this, an' Tommy that, an'
        " Tommy, 'ow's yer soul ? "
    But it's " Thin red line of 'eroes " when the
        drums begin to roll—
    The drums begin to roll, my boys, the drums
        begin to roll,
    O it's " Thin red line of 'eroes " when the
        drums begin to roll.

We aren't no thin red 'eroes, nor we aren't no
    blackguards too,
But single men in barricks, most remarkable like
    you ;
An' if sometimes our conduck isn't all your fancy
    paints,
Why, single men in barricks don't grow into
    plaster saints ;
    While it's Tommy this, an' Tommy that, an'
        " Tommy, fall be'ind,"
    But it's " Please to walk in front, sir," when
        there's trouble in the wind—
    There's trouble in the wind, my boys, there's
        trouble in the wind,
    O it's " Please to walk in front, sir," when
        there's trouble in the wind.

You talk o' better food for us, an' schools, an'
    fires, an all :

We'll wait for extry rations if you treat us rational.
Don't mess about the cook-room slops, but prove
it to our face
The Widow's Uniform is not the soldier-man's
disgrace.

> For it's Tommy this, an' Tommy that, an'
> " Chuck him out, the brute ! "
> But it's " Saviour of 'is country " when the
> guns begin to shoot ;
> An' it's Tommy this, an' Tommy that, an'
> anything you please ;
> An' Tommy ain't a bloomin' fool—you bet
> that Tommy sees !

THE ABSENT-MINDED BEGGAR

WHEN you've shouted " Rule Britannia," when
you've sung " God Save the Queen,"
When you've finished killing Kruger with your
mouth,
Will you kindly drop a shilling in my little
tambourine
For a gentleman in *khaki* ordered South ?
He's an absent-minded beggar, and his weaknesses
are great—
But we and Paul must take him as we find him—
He is out on active service, wiping something off
a slate—
And he's left a lot of little things behind him !
Duke's son—cook's son—son of a hundred kings—

(Fifty thousand horse and foot going to Table
    Bay !)
Each of 'em doing his country's work
    (and who's to look after their things ?)
Pass the hat for your credit's sake,
             and pay—pay—pay !

There are girls he married secret, asking no per-
    mission to,
  For he knew he wouldn't get it if he did.
There is gas and coals and vittles, and the house-
    rent falling due,
  And it's more than rather likely there's a kid.
There are girls he walked with casual. They'll be
    sorry now he's gone,
  For an absent-minded beggar they will find him,
But it ain't the time for sermons with the winter
    coming on.
  We must help the girl that Tommy's left behind
    him !
Cook's son—Duke's son—son of a belted Earl—
  Son of a Lambeth publican—it's all the same
    to-day !
Each of 'em doing his country's work
    (and who's to look after the girl ?)
Pass the hat for your credit's sake,
             and pay—pay—pay !

There are families by thousands, far too proud to
    beg or speak,
  And they'll put their sticks and bedding up the
    spout,

And they'll live on half o' nothing, paid 'em
    punctual once a week,
  'Cause the man that earns the wage is ordered
    out.
He's an absent-minded beggar, but he heard his
    country call,
  And his reg'ment didn't need to send to find
    him !
He chucked his job and joined it—so the job before
    us all
  Is to help the home that Tommy's left behind
    him !
Duke's   job—cook's   job—gardener,   baronet,
    groom,
  Mews or palace or paper-shop, there's someone
    gone away !
Each of 'em doing his country's work
  (and who's to look after the room ?)
Pass the hat for your credit's sake,
              and pay—pay—pay !

Let us manage so as, later, we can look him in the
    face,
  And tell him—what he'd very much prefer—
That, while he saved the Empire, his employer
    saved his place,
  And his mates (that's you and me) looked out
    for *her*.
He's an absent-minded beggar and he may forget
    it all,
  But we do not want his kiddies to remind him

That we sent 'em to the workhouse while their
    daddy hammered Paul,
  So we'll help the homes that Tommy left behind
    him !
Cook's home — Duke's home — home of a
    millionaire,
  (Fifty thousand horse and foot going to Table
    Bay !)
Each of 'em doing his country's work
  (and what have you got to spare ?)
Pass the hat for your credit's sake,
               and pay—pay—pay !

PIET

(Regular of the Line)

I DO not love my Empire's foes,
  Nor call 'em angels ; still,
What *is* the sense of 'atin' those
  'Oom you are paid to kill ?
So, barrin' all that foreign lot
  Which only joined for spite,
Myself, I'd just as soon as not
  Respect the man I fight.
    Ah there, Piet !—'is trousies to 'is knees,
      'Is coat-tails lyin' level in the bullet-sprinkled
        breeze ;
      'E does not lose 'is rifle an' 'e does not lose
        'is seat.
    I've known a lot 'o people ride a dam' sight
      worse than Piet.

I've 'eard 'im cryin' from the ground
    Like Abel's blood of old,
An' skirmished out to look, an' found
    The beggar nearly cold.
I've waited on till 'e was dead
    (Which couldn't 'elp 'im much),
But many grateful things 'e's said
    To me for doin' such.

    Ah there, Piet ! whose time 'as come to die,
      'Is carcase past rebellion, but 'is eyes inquirin'
        why.
    Though dressed in stolen uniform with badge
        o' rank complete,
    I've known a lot o' fellers go a dam' sight
        worse than Piet.

An' when there wasn't aught to do
    But camp and cattle-guards,
I've fought with 'im the 'ole day through
    At fifteen 'undred yards ;
Long afternoons o' lyin' still,
    An' 'earin' as you lay
The bullets swish from 'ill to 'ill
    Like scythes among the 'ay.

    Ah there, Piet !—be'ind 'is stony kop—
    With 'is Boer bread an' biltong,[1] an' 'is flask
        of awful Dop ;[2]
    'Is Mauser for amusement an' 'is pony for
        retreat,
    I've known a lot o' fellers shoot a dam' sight
        worse than Piet.

[1] Dried meat.   [2] Cape brandy.

He's shoved 'is rifle 'neath my nose
    Before I'd time to think,
An' borrowed all my Sunday clo'es
    An' sent me 'ome in pink;
An' I 'ave crept (Lord, 'ow I've crept!)
    On 'ands an' knees I've gone,
And spoored and floored and caught and kept
    An' sent him to Ceylon![1]
        Ah there, Piet!—you've sold me many a pup,
        When week on week alternate it was you an'
            me " 'ands up!"
        But though I never made *you* walk man-
            naked in the 'eat,
        I've known a lot o' fellers stalk a dam' sight
            worse than Piet.

From Plewman's to Marabastad,
    From Ookiep to De Aar,
Me an' my trusty friend 'ave 'ad,
    As you might say, a war;
But seein' what both parties done
    Before 'e owned defeat,
I ain't more proud of 'avin' won,
    Than I am pleased with Piet.
        Ah there, Piet!—picked up be'ind the drive!
        The wonder wasn't 'ow 'e fought, but 'ow 'e
            kep' alive,
        With nothin' in 'is belly, on 'is back, or to 'is
            feet—
        I've known a lot o' men behave a dam' sight
            worse than Piet.

[1] One of the camps for prisoners of this war was in Ceylon.

No more I'll 'ear 'is rifle crack
  Along the block'ouse fence—
The beggar's on the peaceful tack,
  Regardless of expense ;
For countin' what 'e eats an' draws,
  An' gifts an' loans as well,
'E's gettin' 'alf the Earth, because
  'E didn't give us 'Ell !

    Ah there, Piet ! with your brand-new English
      plough,
    Your gratis tents an' cattle, an' your most
      ungrateful frow,
    You've made the British taxpayer rebuild your
      country-seat—
    I've known some pet battalions charge a dam'
      sight less than Piet.

THE WHITE MAN'S BURDEN

1899

    TAKE up the White Man's burden—
      Send forth the best ye breed—
    Go bind your sons to exile
      To serve your captives' need ;
    To wait in heavy harness,
      On fluttered folk and wild—
    Your new-caught, sullen peoples,
      Half-devil and half-child.

Take up the White Man's Burden—
   In patience to abide,
To veil the threat of terror
   And check the show of pride ;
By open speech and simple,
   An hundred times made plain,
To seek another's profit,
   And work another's gain.

Take up the White Man's burden—
   The savage wars of peace—
Fill full the mouth of Famine
   And bid the sickness cease ;
And when your goal is nearest
   The end for others sought,
Watch Sloth and heathen Folly
   Bring all your hope to nought.

Take up the White Man's burden—
   No tawdry rule of kings,
But toil of serf and sweeper—
   The tale of common things.
The ports ye shall not enter,
   The roads ye shall not tread,
Go make them with your living,
   And mark them with your dead !

Take up the White Man's burden—
   And reap his old reward :
The blame of those ye better,
   The hate of those ye guard—

The cry of hosts ye humour
   (Ah, slowly !) toward the light :—
" Why brought ye us from bondage,
  " Our loved Egyptian night ? "

Take up the White Man's burden—
   Ye dare not stoop to less—
Nor call too loud on Freedom
   To cloak your weariness ;
By all ye cry or whisper,
   By all ye leave or do,
The silent, sullen peoples
   Shall weigh your Gods and you.

Take up the White Man's burden—
   Have done with childish days—
The lightly proffered laurel,
   The easy, ungrudged praise.
Comes now, to search your manhood
   Through all the thankless years,
Cold, edged with dear-bought wisdom,
   The judgment of your peers !

THE SONG OF THE WOMEN

(Lady Dufferin's Fund for medical aid to the Women of India)

How shall she know the worship we would do her ?
   The walls are high and she is very far.
How shall the women's message reach unto her
   Above the tumult of the packed bazaar ?

Free wind of March, against the lattice
  blowing,
Bear thou our thanks lest she depart un-
  knowing.

Go forth across the fields we may not roam in,
  Go forth beyond the trees that rim the city
To whatsoe'er fair place she hath her home in,
  Who dowered us with wealth of love and pity.
    Out of our shadow pass and seek her singing—
    " I have no gifts but Love alone for bringing."

Say that we be a feeble folk who greet her,
  But old in grief, and very wise in tears :
Say that we, being desolate, entreat her
  That she forget us not in after-years ;
    For we have seen the light and it were grievous
    To dim that dawning if our Lady leave us.

By Life that ebbed with none to staunch the failing,
  By Love's sad harvest garnered ere the spring,
When Love in Ignorance wept unavailing
  O'er young buds dead before their blossoming ;
    By all the grey owl watched, the pale moon
      viewed,
    In past grim years declare our gratitude !

By hands uplifted to the Gods that heard not,
  By gifts that found no favour in their sight,
By faces bent above the babe that stirred not,
  By nameless horrors of the stifling night ;
    By ills fordone, by peace her toils discover,

Bid Earth be good beneath and Heaven above
her !

If she have sent her servants in our pain,
If she have fought with Death and dulled his
sword ;
If she have given back our sick again,
And to the breast the weakling lips restored,
Is it a little thing that she has wrought ?
Then Life and Death and Motherhood be
nought.

Go forth, O Wind, our message on thy wings,
And they shall hear thee pass and bid thee speed,
In reed-roofed hut, or white-walled home of kings,
Who have been holpen by her in their need.
All spring shall give thee fragrance, and the
wheat
Shall be a tasselled floorcloth to thy feet.

Haste, for our hearts are with thee, take no rest !
Loud-voiced ambassador, from sea to sea
Proclaim the blessing, manifold, confest,
Of those in darkness by her hand set free,
Then very softly to her presence move,
And whisper : " Lady, lo, they know and
love ! "

RECESSIONAL

1897

GOD of our fathers, known of old,
Lord of our far-flung battle-line,

Beneath whose awful Hand we hold
　　Dominion over palm and pine—
Lord God of Hosts, be with us yet,
Lest we forget—lest we forget !

The tumult and the shouting dies ;
　　The Captains and the Kings depart :
Still stands Thine ancient sacrifice,
　　An humble and a contrite heart.
Lord God of Hosts, be with us yet,
Lest we forget—lest we forget !

Far-called, our navies melt away ;
　　On dune and headland sinks the fire :
Lo, all our pomp of yesterday
　　Is one with Nineveh and Tyre !
Judge of the Nations, spare us yet,
Lest we forget—lest we forget !

If, drunk with sight of power, we loose
　　Wild tongues that have not Thee in awe,
Such boastings as the Gentiles use,
　　Or lesser breeds without the Law—
Lord God of Hosts, be with us yet,
Lest we forget—lest we forget !

For heathen heart that puts her trust
　　In reeking tube and iron shard,
All valiant dust that builds on dust,
　　And guarding, calls not Thee to guard,
For frantic boast and foolish word—
Thy mercy on Thy People, Lord !

MEN AND WOMEN

"WHEN 'OMER SMOTE 'IS BLOOMIN' LYRE"

WHEN 'Omer smote 'is bloomin' lyre,
  He'd 'eard men sing by land an' sea;
An' what he thought 'e might require,
  'E went an' took—the same as me!

The market-girls an' fishermen,
  The shepherds an' the sailors, too,
They 'eard old songs turn up again,
  But kep' it quiet—same as you!

They knew 'e stole; 'e knew they knowed.
  They didn't tell, nor make a fuss,
But winked at 'Omer down the road,
  An' 'e winked back—the same as us!

THE LADIES

I'VE taken my fun where I've found it;
  I've rogued an' I've ranged in my time;
I've 'ad my pickin' o' sweethearts,
  An' four o' the lot was prime.
One was an 'arf-caste widow,
  One was a woman at Prome,
One was the wife of a *jemadar-sais*,[1]
  An' one is a girl at 'ome.

Now I aren't no 'and with the ladies,
  For, takin' 'em all along,
You never can say till you've tried 'em,
  An' then you are like to be wrong.

[1] Head-groom.

63

There's times when you'll think that you mightn't,
  There's times when you'll know that you might ,
But the things you will learn from the Yellow an' Brown,
  They'll 'elp you a lot with the White !

I was a young un at 'Oogli,
  Shy as a girl to begin ;
Aggie de Castrer she made me,
  An' Aggie was clever as sin ;
Older than me, but my first un—
  More like a mother she were—
Showed me the way to promotion an' pay,
  An' I learned about women from 'er !

Then I was ordered to Burma,
  Actin' in charge o' Bazar,
An' I got me a tiddy live 'eathen
  Through buyin' supplies off 'er pa.
Funny an' yellow an' faithful—
  Doll in a teacup she were—
But we lived on the square, like a true-married pair,
  An' I learned about women from 'er !

Then we was shifted to Neemuch
  (Or I might ha' been keepin' 'er now),
An' I took with a shiny she-devil,
  The wife of a nigger at Mhow ;
'Taught me the gipsy-folks' *bolee* ;[1]
  Kind o' volcano she were,
For she knifed me one night 'cause I wished she
      was white,
  And I learned about women from 'er !

[1] Slang.

64

Then I come 'ome in a trooper,
   'Long of a kid o' sixteen—
'Girl from a convent at Meerut,
   The straightest I ever 'ave seen.
Love at first sight was 'er trouble,
   She didn't know what it were ;
An' I wouldn't do such, 'cause I liked 'er too much,
   But—I learned about women from 'er !

I've taken my fun where I've found it,
   An' now I must pay for my fun,
For the more you 'ave known o' the others
   The less will you settle to one ;
An' the end of it's sittin' and thinkin',
   An' dreamin' Hell-fires to see ;
So be warned by my lot (which I know you will
      not),
   An' learn about women from me !

What did the Colonel's Lady think ?
   Nobody never knew.
Somebody asked the Sergeant's Wife,
   An' she told 'em true !
When you get to a man in the case,
   They're like as a row of pins—
For the Colonel's Lady an' Judy O'Grady
   Are sisters under their skins !

"RIMINI"

(Marching Song of a Roman Legion of the Later Empire)

WHEN I left Rome for Lalage's sake,
By the Legions' Road to Rimini,
She vowed her heart was mine to take
With me and my shield to Rimini—
(Till the Eagles flew from Rimini—)
And I've tramped Britain, and I've tramped Gaul,
And the Pontic shore where the snow-flakes fall
As white as the neck of Lalage—
(As cold as the heart of Lalage!)
And I've lost Britain, and I've lost Gaul,
And I've lost Rome and, worst of all,
I've lost Lalage!

When you go by the Via Aurelia,
As thousands have travelled before,
Remember the Luck of the Soldier
Who never saw Rome any more!
Oh dear was the sweetheart that kissed him,
And dear was the mother that bore;
But his shield was picked up in the heather,
And he never saw Rome any more!

And *he* left Rome, etc.

When you go by the Via Aurelia
That runs from the City to Gaul,
Remember the Luck of the Soldier
Who rose to be master of all!

He carried the sword and the buckler,
He mounted his guard on the Wall,
Till the Legions elected him Cæsar,
And he rose to be master of all !

And *he* left Rome, etc.

It's twenty-five marches to Narbo,
It's forty-five more up the Rhone,
And the end may be death in the heather
Or life on an Emperor's throne.
But whether the Eagles obey us,
Or we go to the Ravens—alone,
I'd sooner be Lalage's lover
Than sit on an Emperor's throne !

We've *all* left Rome for Lalage's sake, etc.

THE VAMPIRE

1897

A FOOL there was and he made his prayer
(Even as you and I !)
To a rag and a bone and a hank of hair
(We called her the woman who did not care)
But the fool he called her his lady fair—
(Even as you and I !)

Oh, the years we waste and the tears we waste
And the work of our head and hand
Belong to the woman who did not know
(And now we know that she never could know)
And did not understand !

A fool there was and his goods he spent
(Even as you and I !)
Honour and faith and a sure intent
(And it wasn't the least what the lady meant)
But a fool must follow his natural bent
(Even as you and I !)

Oh, the toil we lost and the spoil we lost
And the excellent things we planned
Belong to the woman who didn't know why
(And now we know that she never knew why)
And did not understand !

The fool was stripped to his foolish hide
(Even as you and I !)
Which she might have seen when she threw him
aside—
(But it isn't on record the lady tried)
So some of him lived but the most of him died—
(Even as you and I !)

And it isn't the shame and it isn't the blame
That stings like a white hot brand—
It's coming to know that she never knew why
(Seeing, at last, she could never know why)
And never could understand !

TOMLINSON

1891

Now Tomlinson gave up the ghost at his house in
Berkeley Square,
And a Spirit came to his bedside and gripped him
by the hair—

A Spirit gripped him by the hair and carried him
    far away,
Till he heard as the roar of a rain-fed ford the roar
    of the Milky Way :
Till he heard the roar of the Milky Way die down
    and drone and cease,
And they came to the Gate within the Wall where
    Peter holds the keys.
" Stand up, stand up now, Tomlinson, and answer
    loud and high
" The good that ye did for the sake of men or ever
    ye came to die—
" The good that ye did for the sake of men on little
    earth so lone ! "
And the naked soul of Tomlinson grew white as a
    rain-washed bone.
" O I have a friend on earth," he said, " that was
    my priest and guide,
" And well would he answer all for me if he were
    at my side."
—" For that ye strove in neighbour-love it shall
    be written fair,
" But now ye wait at Heaven's Gate and not in
    Berkeley Square :
" Though we called your friend from his bed this
    night, he could not speak for you,
" For the race is run by one and one and never by
    two and two."
Then Tomlinson looked up and down, and little
    gain was there,

For the naked stars grinned overhead, and he saw
    that his soul was bare.
The Wind that blows between the Worlds, it cut
    him like a knife,
And Tomlinson took up the tale and spoke of his
    good in life.
" O this I have read in a book," he said, " and that
    was told to me,
" And this I have thought that another man
    thought of a Prince in Muscovy."
The good souls flocked like homing doves and
    bade him clear the path,
And Peter twirled the jangling Keys in weariness
    and wrath.
" Ye have read, ye have heard, ye have thought,"
    he said, " and the tale is yet to run :
" By the worth of the body that once ye had, give
    answer—what ha' ye done ? "
Then Tomlinson looked back and forth, and little
    good it bore,
For the darkness stayed at his shoulder-blade and
    Heaven's Gate before :—
" O this I have felt, and this I have guessed, and
    this I have heard men say,
" And this they wrote that another man wrote of a
    carl in Norroway."
" Ye have read, ye have felt, ye have guessed,
    good lack ! Ye have hampered Heaven's
    Gate ;
" There's little room between the stars in idleness
    to prate !

" O none may reach by hired speech of neighbour,
        priest, and kin
" Through borrowed deed to God's good meed
        that lies so fair within ;
" Get hence, get hence to the Lord of Wrong, for
        the doom has yet to run,
" And . . . the faith that ye share with Berkeley
        Square uphold you, Tomlinson ! "

.   .   .   .   .

The Spirit gripped him by the hair, and sun by
        sun they fell
Till they came to the belt of Naughty Stars that
        rim the mouth of Hell.
The first are red with pride and wrath, the next are
        white with pain,
But the third are black with clinkered sin that
        cannot burn again.
They may hold their path, they may leave their
        path, with never a soul to mark :
They may burn or freeze, but they must not cease
        in the Scorn of the Outer Dark.
The Wind that blows between the Worlds, it
        nipped him to the bone,
And he yearned to the flare of Hell-gate there as
        the light of his own hearth-stone.
The Devil he sat behind the bars, where the des-
        perate legions drew,
But he caught the hasting Tomlinson and would
        not let him through.
" Wot ye the price of good pit-coal that I must
        pay ? " said he,

" That ye rank yoursel' so fit for Hell and ask no
      leave of me ?

" I am all o'er-sib to Adam's breed that ye should
      give me scorn,

" For I strove with God for your First Father the
      day that he was born.

" Sit down, sit down upon the slag, and answer
      loud and high

" The harm that ye did to the Sons of Men or ever
      you came to die."

And Tomlinson looked up and up, and saw against
      the night

The belly of a tortured star blood-red in Hell-
      Mouth light ;

And Tomlinson looked down and down, and saw
      beneath his feet

The frontlet of a tortured star milk-white in Hell-
      Mouth heat.

" O I had a love on earth," said he, " that kissed
      me to my fall ;

" And if ye would call my love to me I know she
      would answer all."

—" All that ye did in love forbid it shall be written
      fair,

" But now ye wait at Hell-Mouth Gate and not in
      Berkeley Square :

" Though we whistled your love from her bed
      to-night, I trow she would not run,

" For the sin ye do by two and two ye must pay
      for one by one ! "

The Wind that blows between the Worlds, it cut
    him like a knife,

And Tomlinson took up the tale and spoke of his
    sins in life :—

" Once I ha' laughed at the power of Love and
    twice at the grip of the Grave,

" And thrice I ha' patted my God on the head that
    men might call me brave."

The Devil he blew on a brandered soul and set it
    aside to cool :—

" Do ye think I would waste my good pit-coal on
    the hide of a brain-sick fool ?

" I see no worth in the hobnailed mirth or the
    jolthead jest ye did

" That I should waken my gentlemen that are
    sleeping three on a grid."

Then Tomlinson looked back and forth, and there
    was little grace.

For Hell-Gate filled the houseless soul with the
    Fear of Naked Space.

" Nay, this I ha' heard," quo' Tomlinson, " and
    this was noised abroad,

" And this I ha' got from a Belgian book on the
    word of a dead French lord."

—" Ye ha' heard, ye ha' read, ye ha' got, good
    lack ! and the tale begins afresh—

" Have ye sinned one sin for the pride o' the eye
    or the sinful lust of the flesh ? "

Then Tomlinson he gripped the bars and yam-
    mered, " Let me in—

"For I mind that I borrowed my neighbour's wife
    to sin the deadly sin."

The Devil he grinned behind the bars, and banked
    the fires high :

"Did ye read of that sin in a book ? " said he ;
    and Tomlinson said, " Ay ! "

The Devil he blew upon his nails, and the little
    devils ran,

And he said : " Go husk this whimpering thief
    that comes in the guise of a man :

"Winnow him out 'twixt star and star, and sieve
    his proper worth :

"There's sore decline in Adam's line if this be
    spawn of earth."

Empusa's crew, so naked-new they may not face
    the fire,

But weep that they bin too small to sin to the
    height of their desire,

Over the coal they chased the Soul, and racked it
    all abroad,

As children rifle a caddis-case or the raven's foolish
    hoard.

And back they came with the tattered Thing, as
    children after play,

And they said : " The soul that he got from God
    he has bartered clean away.

"We have threshed a stook of print and book,
    and winnowed a chattering wind,

"And many a soul wherefrom he stole, but his
    we cannot find.

" We have handled him, we have dandled him, we
    have seared him to the bone,
" And Sire, if tooth and nail show truth he has no
    soul of his own."
The Devil he bowed his head on his breast and
    rumbled deep and low :—
" I'm all o'er-sib to Adam's breed that I should
    bid him go.
" Yet close we lie, and deep we lie, and if I gave
    him place,
" My gentlemen that are so proud would flout me
    to my face ;
" They'd call my house a common stews and me a
    careless host,
" And—I would not anger my gentlemen for the
    sake of a shiftless ghost."
The Devil he looked at the mangled Soul that
    prayed to feel the flame,
And he thought of Holy Charity, but he thought
    of his own good name :—
" Now ye could haste my coal to waste, and sit ye
    down to fry.
" Did ye think of that theft for yourself ? " said he ;
    and Tomlinson said, " Ay ! "
The Devil he blew an outward breath, for his heart
    was free from care :—
" Ye have scarce the soul of a louse," he said,
    " but the roots of sin are there.
" And for that sin should ye come in were I the
    lord alone,

" But sinful pride has rule inside—ay, mightier
    than my own.

" Honour and Wit, fore-damned they sit, to each
    his Priest and Whore ;

" Nay, scarce I dare myself go there, and you they'd
    torture sore.

" Ye are neither spirit nor spirk," he said ; " ye
    are neither book nor brute—

" Go, get ye back to the flesh again for the sake of
    Man's repute.

" I'm all o'er-sib to Adam's breed that I should
    mock your pain,

" But look that ye win to worthier sin ere ye come
    back again.

" Get hence, the hearse is at your door—the grim
    black stallions wait—

" They bear your clay to place to-day. Speed,
    lest ye come too late !

" Go back to Earth with a lip unsealed—go back
    with an open eye,

" And carry my word to the Sons of Men or ever
    ye come to die :

" That the sin they do by two and two they must
    pay for one by one,

" And . . . the God, that you took from a printed
    book be with you, Tomlinson ! "

PAGETT, M.P.

The toad beneath the harrow knows
Exactly where each tooth-point goes ;
The butterfly upon the road
Preaches contentment to that toad.

PAGETT, M.P., was a liar, and a fluent liar therewith,—

He spoke of the heat of India as " The Asian Solar Myth " ;

'Came on a four months' visit, to " study the East " in November,

And I got him to make an agreement vowing to stay till September.

March came in with the *köil*. Pagett was cool and gay,

Called me a " bloated Brahmin," talked of my " princely pay."

March went out with the roses. " Where is your heat ? " said he.

" Coming," said I to Pagett. " Skittles ! " said Pagett, M.P.

April began with the punkah, coolies, and prickly-heat,—

Pagett was dear to mosquitoes, sandflies found him a treat.

He grew speckled and lumpy—hammered, I grieve to say,

Aryan brothers who fanned him, in an illiberal way.

May set in with a dust-storm,—Pagett went down
 with the sun.
All the delights of the season tickled him one by
 one.
Imprimis—ten days' " liver "—due to his drinking
 beer ;
Later, a dose of fever—slight, but he called it
 severe.

Dysent'ry touched him in June, after the *Chota
 Bursat*[1]—
Lowered his portly person—made him yearn to
 depart.
He didn't call me a " Brahmin," or " bloated," or
 " over-paid,"
But seemed to think it a wonder that any one ever
 stayed.

July was a trifle unhealthy,—Pagett was ill with
 fear,
Called it the " Cholera Morbus," hinted that life
 was dear.
He babbled of " Eastern exile," and mentioned his
 home with tears ;
But I hadn't seen *my* children for close upon seven
 years.

We reached a hundred and twenty once in the
 Court at noon,
[I've mentioned Pagett was portly] Pagett went
 off in a swoon.

<hr>

[1] The early rains.

That was an end to the business. Pagett, the
    perjured, fled
With a practical, working knowledge of " Solar
    Myths " in his head.

And I laughed as I drove from the station, but the
    mirth died out on my lips
As I thought of the fools like Pagett who write
    of their " Eastern trips,"
And the sneers of the travelled idiots who duly
    misgovern the land,
And I prayed to the Lord to deliver another one
    into my hand.

M'ANDREW'S HYMN

1893

LORD, Thou hast made this world below the
    shadow of a dream,
An', taught by time, I tak' it so—exceptin' always
    Steam.
From coupler-flange to spindle-guide I see Thy
    Hand, O God—
Predestination in the stride o' yon connectin'-rod.
John Calvin might ha' forged the same—enorr-
    mous, certain, slow—
Ay, wrought it in the furnace-flame—*my*
    " Institutio."
I cannot get my sleep to-night; old bones are
    hard to please;

I'll stand the middle watch up here—alone wi' God
    an' these

My engines, after ninety days o' race an' rack an'
    strain

Through all the seas of all Thy world, slam-bangin'
    home again.

Slam-bang too much—they knock a wee—the
    crosshead-gibs are loose,

But thirty thousand mile o' sea has gied them fair
    excuse. . . .

Fine, clear an' dark—a full-draught breeze, wi'
    Ushant out o' sight,

An' Ferguson relievin' Hay. Old girl, ye'll walk
    to-night !

His wife's at Plymouth. . . . Seventy—One—
    Two—Three since he began—

Three turns for Mistress Ferguson . . . and who's
    to blame the man ?

There's none at any port for me, by drivin' fast
    or slow,

Since Elsie Campbell went to Thee, Lord, thirty
    years ago.

(The year the *Sarah Sands* was burned. Oh roads
    we used to tread,

Fra' Maryhill to Pollokshaws—fra' Govan to
    Parkhead !)

Not but they're ceevil on the Board. Ye'll hear
    Sir Kenneth say :

" Good morrn, McAndrew ! Back again ? An'
    how's your bilge to-day ? "

Miscallin' technicalities but handin' me my chair

To drink Madeira wi' three Earls—the auld Fleet
    Engineer

That started as a boiler-whelp—when steam and
    he were low.

I mind the time we used to serve a broken pipe wi'
    tow !

Ten pound was all the pressure then—Eh ! Eh !
    —a man wad drive ;

An' here, our workin' gauges give one hunder
    sixty-five !

We're creepin' on wi' each new rig—less weight
    an' larger power ;

There'll be the loco-boiler next an' thirty mile an
    hour !

Thirty an' more. What I ha' seen since ocean-
    steam began

Leaves me na doot for the machine : but what
    about the man ?

The man that counts, wi' all his runs, one million
    mile o' sea :

Four time the span from earth to moon. . . . How
    far, O Lord, from Thee

That wast beside him night an' day ? Ye mind
    my first typhoon ?

It scoughed the skipper on his way to jock wi' the
    saloon.

Three feet were on the stokehold-floor—just
    slappin' to an' fro—

An' cast me on a furnace-door. I have the marks
    to show.

Marks ! I ha' marks o' more than burns—deep
in my soul an' black,
An' times like this, when things go smooth, my
wickudness comes back.
The sins o' four an' forty years, all up an' down
the seas,
Clack an' repeat like valves half-fed. . . . Forgie's
our trespasses !
Nights when I'd come on deck to mark, wi' envy
in my gaze,
The couples kittlin' in the dark between the
funnel-stays ;
Years when I raked the Ports wi' pride to fill my
cup o' wrong—
Judge not, O Lord, my steps aside at Gay Street
in Hong-Kong !
Blot out the wastrel hours of mine in sin when I
abode—
Jane Harrigan's an' Number Nine, The Reddick
an' Grant Road !
An' waur than all—my crownin' sin—rank blas-
phemy an' wild.
I was not four and twenty then—Ye wadna judge
a child ?
I'd seen the Tropics first that run—new fruit, new
smells, new air—
How could I tell—blind-fou wi' sun—the Deil
was lurkin' there ?
By day like playhouse-scenes the shore slid past
our sleepy eyes ;

By night those soft, lasceevious stars leered from
    those velvet skies,
In port (we used no cargo-steam) I'd daunder down
    the streets—
An ijjit grinnin' in a dream—for shells an' parra-
    keets,
An' walkin'-sticks o' carved bamboo an' blowfish
    stuffed an' dried—
Fillin' my bunk wi' rubbishry the Chief put
    overside.
Till, off Sambawa Head, Ye mind, I heard a land-
    breeze ca',
Milk-warm wi' breath o' spice an' bloom:
    " McAndrew, come awa' ! "
Firm, clear an' low—no haste, no hate—the
    ghostly whisper went,
Just statin' eevidential facts beyon' all argument :
" Your mither's God's a graspin' deil, the shadow
    o' yoursel',
" Got out o' books by meenisters clean daft on
    Heaven an' Hell.
" They mak' him in the Broomielaw, o' Glasgie
    cold an' dirt,
" A jealous, pridefu' fetich, lad, that's only strong
    to hurt.
" Ye'll not go back to Him again an' kiss His red-
    hot rod,
" But come wi' Us " (Now, who were *They* ?)
    " an' know the Leevin' God,
" That does not kipper souls for sport or break a
    life in jest,

" But swells the ripenin' cocoanuts an' ripes the
    woman's breast."

An' there it stopped—cut off—no more—that quiet,
    certain voice—

For me, six months o' twenty-four, to leave or take
    at choice.

'Twas on me like a thunderclap—it racked me
    through an' through—

Temptation past the show o' speech, unnameable
    an' new—

The Sin against the Holy Ghost ? . . . An' under
    all, our screw.

That storm blew by but left behind her anchor-
    shiftin' swell.

Thou knowest all my heart an' mind, Thou
    knowest, Lord, I fell—

Third on the *Mary Gloster* then, and first that night
    in Hell !

Yet was Thy Hand beneath my head, about my
    feet Thy Care—

Fra' Deli clear to Torres Strait, the trial o' despair,

But when we touched the Barrier Reef Thy answer
    to my prayer ! . . .

We dared na run that sea by night but lay an' held
    our fire,

An' I was drowsin' on the hatch—sick—sick wi'
    doubt an' tire :

" *Better the sight of eyes that see than wanderin' o'*
    desire ! "

Ye mind that word? Clear as our gongs—again,
    an' once again,
When rippin' down through coral-trash ran out
    our moorin'-chain :
An', by Thy Grace, I had the Light to see my duty
    plain.
Light on the engine-room—no more—bright as
    our carbons burn.
I've lost it since a thousand times, but never past
    return !

    •   •   •   •   •

Obsairve! Per annum we'll have here two
    thousand souls aboard—
Think not I dare to justify myself before the Lord,
But—average fifteen hunder souls safe-borne fra'
    port to port—
I *am* o' service to my kind. Ye wadna blame the
    thought ?
Maybe they steam from Grace to Wrath—to sin
    by folly led—
It isna mine to judge their path—their lives are on
    my head.
Mine at the last—when all is done it all comes back
    to me,
The fault that leaves six thousand ton a log upon
    the sea.
We'll tak' one stretch—three weeks an' odd by
    ony road ye steer—
Fra' Cape Town east to Wellington—ye need an
    engineer.

Fail there—ye've time to weld your shaft—ay, eat
it, ere ye're spoke ;

Or make Kerguelen under sail—three jiggers
burned wi' smoke !

An' home again—the Rio run : it's no child's
play to go

Steamin' to bell for fourteen days o' snow an' floe
an' blow.

The bergs like kelpies overside that girn an' turn
an' shift

Whaur, grindin' like the Mills o' God, goes by the
big South drift.

(Hail, Snow and Ice that praise the Lord. I've
met them at their work,

An' wished we had anither route or they anither
kirk.)

Yon's strain, hard strain, o' head an' hand, for
though Thy Power brings

All skill to naught, Ye'll understand a man must
think o' things.

Then, at the last, we'll get to port an' hoist their
baggage clear—

The passengers, wi' gloves an' canes—an' this is
what I'll hear :

" Well, thank ye for a pleasant voyage. The
tender's comin' now."

While I go testin' follower-bolts an' watch the
skipper bow.

They've words for every one but me—shake hands
wi' half the crew,

Except the dour Scots engineer, the man they never
      knew.
An' yet I like the wark for all we've dam'-few
      pickin's here—
No pension, an' the most we'll earn's four hunder
      pound a year.
Better myself abroad? Maybe. *I'd* sooner starve
      than sail
Wi' such as call a snifter-rod *ross*. . . . French for
      nightingale.
Commeesion on my stores? Some do; but I
      cannot afford
To lie like stewards wi' patty-pans. I'm older
      than the Board.
A bonus on the coal I save? Ou ay, the Scots
      are close,
But when I grudge the strength Ye gave I'll grudge
      their food to *those*.
(There's bricks that I might recommend—an'
      clink the fire-bars cruel.
No! Welsh—Wangarti at the worst—an' damn
      all patent fuel!)
Inventions? Ye must stay in port to mak' a
      patent pay.
My Deeferential Valve-Gear taught me how that
      business lay.
I blame no chaps wi' clearer heads for aught they
      make or sell.
I found that I could not invent an' look to these
      as well.

So, wrestled wi' Apollyon—Nah !—fretted like a
  bairn—
But burned the workin'-plans last run, wi' all I
  hoped to earn.
Ye know how hard an Idol dies, an' what that
  meant to me—
E'en tak' it for a sacrifice acceptable to Thee. . . .
*Below there ! Oiler ! What's your wark ? Ye find
  it runnin' hard ?*
Ye needn't swill the cup wi' oil—this isn't the Cunard !
*Ye thought ? Ye are not paid to think. Go, sweat
  that off again !*
Tck ! Tck ! It's deeficult to sweer nor tak' The
  Name in vain !
Men, ay an' women, call me stern. Wi' these to
  oversee,
Ye'll note I've little time to burn on social repartee.
The bairns see what their elders miss ; they'll hunt
  me to an' fro,
Till for the sake of—well, a kiss—I tak' 'em down
  below.
That minds me of our Viscount loon—Sir
  Kenneth's kin—the chap
Wi' Russia leather tennis-shoon an' spar-decked
  yachtin'-cap.
I showed him round last week, o'er all—an' at the
  last says he :
" Mister McAndrew, don't you think steam spoils
  romance at sea ? "
Damned ijjit ! I'd been doon that morn to see
  what ailed the throws,

Manholin', on my back—the cranks three inches
    off my nose.

Romance! Those first-class passengers they like
    it very well,

Printed an' bound in little books; but why don't
    poets tell?

I'm sick of all their quirks an' turns—the loves an'
    doves they dream—

Lord, send a man like Robbie Burns to sing the
    Song o' Steam!

To match wi Scotia's noblest speech yon orchestra
    sublime

Whaurto—uplifted like the Just—the tail-rods
    mark the time.

The crank-throws give the double-bass, the feed-
    pump sobs an' heaves,

An' now the main eccentrics start their quarrel
    on the sheaves:

Her time, her own appointed time, the rocking
    link-head bides,

Till—hear that note?—the rod's return whings
    glimmerin' through the guides.

They're all awa'! True beat, full power, the
    clangin' chorus goes

Clear to the tunnel where they sit, my purrin'
    dynamoes.

Interdependence absolute, foreseen, ordained,
    decreed,

To work, Ye'll note, at ony tilt an' every rate o'
    speed.

Fra' skylight-lift to furnace-bars, backed, bolted,
    braced an' stayed.

An' singin' like the Mornin' Stars for joy that they
    are made ;

While, out o' touch o' vanity, the sweatin' thrust-
    block says :

" Not unto us the praise, or man—not unto us the
    praise ! "

Now, a' together, hear them lift their lesson—
    theirs an' mine :

" Law, Orrder, Duty an' Restraint, Obedience,
    Discipline ! "

Mill, forge an' try-pit taught them that when
    roarin' they arose,

An' whiles I wonder if a soul was gied them wi'
    the blows.

Oh for a man to weld it then, in one trip-hammer
    strain,

Till even first-class passengers could tell the
    meanin' plain !

But no one cares except mysel' that serve an'
    understand

My seven thousand horse-power here. Eh, Lord !
    They're grand—they're grand !

Uplift am I ? When first in store the new-made
    beasties stood,

Were Ye cast down that breathed the Word
    declarin' all things good ?

Not so ! O' that warld-liftin' joy no after-fall
    could vex,

Ye've left a glimmer still to cheer the Man—the
Arrtifex !
That holds, in spite o' knock and scale, o' friction,
waste an' slip,
An' by that light—now, mark my word—we'll
build the Perfect Ship.
I'll never last to judge her lines or take her curve—
not I.
But I ha' lived an' I ha' worked. Be thanks to
Thee, Most High !
An' I ha' done what I ha' done—judge Thou if
ill or well—
Always Thy Grace preventin' me. . . .
Losh ! Yon's the " Stand-by " bell.
Pilot so soon ? His flare it is. The mornin'-
watch is set.
Well, God be thanked, as I was sayin', I'm no
Pelagian yet.
Now I'll tak' on. . . .
'Morrn, Ferguson. Man, have ye ever thought
What your good leddy costs in coal . . . I'll burn
'em down to port.

MULHOLLAND'S CONTRACT

1894

THE fear was on the cattle, for the gale was on the sea,
An' the pens broke up on the lower deck an' let
the creatures free—
An' the lights went out on the lower deck, an' no
one near but me.

I had been singin' to them to keep 'em quiet there,
For the lower deck is the dangerousest, requirin'
  constant care,
An' give to me as the strongest man, though used
  to drink and swear.

I seed my chance was certain of bein' horned or
  trod,
For the lower deck was packed with steers thicker'n
  peas in a pod,
An' more pens broke at every roll—so I made a
  Contract with God.

An' by the terms of the Contract, as I have read the
  same,
If He got me to port alive I would exalt His Name,
An' praise His Holy Majesty till further orders
  came.

He saved me from the cattle an' He saved me
  from the sea,
For they found me 'tween two drownded ones
  where the roll had landed me—
An' a four-inch crack on top of my head, as crazy
  as could be.

But that were done by a stanchion, an' not by a
  bullock at all,
An' I lay still for seven weeks convalescing of the
  fall,
An' readin' the shiny Scripture texts in the Seaman's
  Hospital.

An' I spoke to God of our Contract, an' He says
    to my prayer :
" I never puts on My ministers no more than they
    can bear.
" So back you go to the cattle-boats an' preach
    My Gospel there.

" For human life is chancy at any kind of trade,
" But most of all, as well you know, when the
    steers are mad-afraid ;
" So you go back to the cattle-boats an' preach
    'em as I've said.

" They must quit drinkin' an' swearin', they
    mustn't knife on a blow,
" They must quit gamblin' their wages, and you
    must preach it so ;
" For now those boats are more like Hell than
    anything else I know."

I didn't want to do it, for I knew what I should
    get ;
An' I wanted to preach Religion, handsome an'
    out of the wet ;
But the Word of the Lord were laid on me, an'
    I done what I was set.

I have been smit an' bruisèd, as warned would
    be the case,
An' turned my cheek to the smiter exactly as
    Scripture says ;
But, following that, I knocked him down an' led
    him up to Grace.

An' we have preaching on Sundays whenever the
    sea is calm,
An' I use no knife or pistol an' I never take no
    harm;
For the Lord abideth back of me to guide my
    fighting arm.

An' I sign for four-pound-ten a month and save
    the money clear,
An' I am in charge of the lower deck, an' I never
    lose a steer;
An' I believe in Almighty God an' I preach His
    Gospel here.

The skippers say I'm crazy, but I can prove 'em
    wrong,
For I am in charge of the lower deck with all that
    doth belong—
Which they would not give to a lunatic, and the com-
    petition so strong!

GUNGA DIN

You may talk o' gin and beer
When you're quartered safe out 'ere,
An' you're sent to penny-fights an' Aldershot it;
But when it comes to slaughter
You will do your work on water,
An' you'll lick the bloomin' boots of 'im that's
    got it.
Now in Injia's sunny clime,
Where I used to spend my time
A-servin' of 'Er Majesty the Queen,

Of all them blackfaced crew
The finest man I knew
Was our regimental bhisti, Gunga Din.
   He was " Din ! Din ! Din !
 " You limpin' lump o' brick-dust, Gunga Din !
   " Hi ! Slippy *bitherao !*
   " Water, get it ! *Panee lao*[1]
 " You squidgy-nosed old idol, Gunga Din."

The uniform 'e wore
Was nothin' much before,
An' rather less than 'arf o' that be'ind,
For a piece o' twisty rag
An' a goatskin water-bag
Was all the field-equipment 'e could find.
When the sweatin' troop-train lay
In a sidin' through the day,
Where the 'eat would make your bloomin'
  eyebrows crawl,
We shouted " Harry By ! "[2]
Till our throats were bricky-dry,
Then we wopped 'im 'cause 'e couldn't serve us
  all.
   It was " Din ! Din ! Din !
 " You 'eathen, where the mischief 'ave you been ?
   " You put some *juldee*[3] in it
   " Or I'll *marrow*[4] you this minute
 " If you don't fill up my helmet, Gunga Din ! "

'E would dot an' carry one
Till the longest day was done ;

[1] Bring water swiftly. [2] O Brother. [3] Be quick. [4] Hit you.

An' 'e didn't seem to know the use o' fear.
If we charged or broke or cut,
You could bet your bloomin' nut,
'E'd be waitin' fifty paces right flank rear.
With 'is mussick[1] on 'is back,
'E would skip with our attack,
An' watch us till the bugles made " Retire,"
An' for all 'is dirty 'ide
'E was white, clear white, inside
When 'e went to tend the wounded under fire !
       It was " Din ! Din ! Din ! "
  With the bullets kickin' dust-spots on the green
      When the cartridges ran out,
        You could hear the front-ranks shout,
  " Hi !   ammunition-mules an' Gunga Din ! "

I shan't forgit the night
When I dropped be'ind the fight
With a bullet where my belt-plate should 'a' been.
I was chokin' mad with thirst,
An' the man that spied me first
Was our good old grinnin', gruntin' Gunga Din.
'E lifted up my 'ead,
An' he plugged me where I bled,
An' 'e guv me 'arf-a-pint o' water green.
It was crawlin' and it stunk,
But of all the drinks I've drunk,
I'm gratefullest to one from Gunga Din.
     . It was " Din ! Din ! Din !
  " 'Ere's a beggar with a bullet through 'is spleen ;

---

[1] Water-skin.

" 'E's chawin' up the ground,
" An' 'e's kickin' all around :
" For Gawd's sake git the water, Gunga Din ! "

'E carried me away
To where a dooli lay,
An' a bullet come an' drilled the beggar clean.
'E put me safe inside,
An' just before 'e died,
" I 'ope you liked your drink," sez Gunga Din.
So I'll meet 'im later on
At the place where 'e is gone—
Where it's always double drill and no canteen.
'E'll be squattin' on the coals
Givin' drink to poor damned souls,
An' I'll get a swig in hell from Gunga Din !
        Yes, Din ! Din ! Din !
    You Lazarushian-leather Gunga Din !
            Though I've belted you and flayed you,
            By the livin' Gawd that made you,
        You're a better man than I am, Gunga Din !

THE BALLAD OF EAST AND WEST

1889

OH, *EAST is East, and West is West, and never the
        twain shall meet,*
*Till Earth and Sky stand presently at God's great
        Judgment Seat ;*

But there is neither East nor West, Border, nor Breed,
nor Birth,
When two strong men stand face to face, though they
come from the ends of the earth !

Kamal is out with twenty men to raise the Border
side,
And he has lifted the Colonel's mare that is the
Colonel's pride.
He has lifted her out of the stable-door between
the dawn and the day,
And turned the calkins upon her feet, and ridden
her far away.
Then up and spoke the Colonel's son that led a
troop of the Guides :
" Is there never a man of all my men can say where
Kamal hides ? "
Then up and spoke Mohammed Khan, the son of
the Ressaldar :
" If ye know the track of the morning-mist, ye
know where his pickets are.
" At dusk he harries the Abazai—at dawn he is
into Bonair,
" But he must go by Fort Bukloh to his own place
to fare.
" So if ye gallop to Fort Bukloh as fast as a bird
can fly,
" By the favour of God ye may cut him off ere he
win to the Tongue of Jagai.
" But if he be past the Tongue of Jagai, right
swiftly turn ye then,

"For the length and the breadth of that
    grisly plain is sown with Kamal's
    men.
"There is rock to the left, and rock to the right,
    and low lean thorn between,
"And ye may hear a breech-bolt snick where never
    a man is seen."
The Colonel's son has taken horse, and a raw
    rough dun was he,
With the mouth of a bell and the heart of Hell and
    the head of a gallows-tree.
The Colonel's son to the Fort has won, they bid
    him stay to eat—
Who rides at the tail of a Border thief, he sits not
    long at his meat.
He's up and away from Fort Bukloh as fast as he
    can fly,
Till he was aware of his father's mare in the gut
    of the Tongue of Jagai,
Till he was aware of his father's mare with Kamal
    upon her back,
And when he could spy the white of her eye, he
    made the pistol crack.
He has fired once, he has fired twice, but the
    whistling ball went wide.
"Ye shoot like a soldier," Kamal said. "Show
    now if ye can ride!"
It's up and over the Tongue of Jagai, as blown
    dust-devils go,
The dun he fled like a stag of ten, but the mare
    like a barren doe.

The dun he leaned against the bit and slugged his
    head above,
But the red mare played with the snaffle-bars, as a
    maiden plays with a glove.
There was rock to the left and rock to the right,
    and low lean thorn between,
And thrice he heard a breech-bolt snick tho' never
    a man was seen.
They have ridden the low moon out of the sky,
    their hoofs drum up the dawn,
The dun he went like a wounded bull, but the
    mare like a new-roused fawn.
The dun he fell at a water-course—in a woeful
    heap fell he,
And Kamal has turned the red mare back, and
    pulled the rider free.
He has knocked the pistol out of his hand—small
    room was there to strive,
" 'Twas only by favour of mine," quoth he, " ye
    rode so long alive :
" There was not a rock for twenty-mile, there
    was not a clump of tree,
" But covered a man of my own men with his
    rifle cocked on his knee.
"If I had raised my bridle-hand, as I have held it low,
" The little jackals that flee so fast were feasting
    all in a row.
" If I had bowed my head on my breast, as I have
    held it high,
" The kite that whistles above us now were gorged
    till she could not fly."

Lightly answered the Colonel's son : " Do good
    to bird and beast,
" But count who come for the broken meats
    before thou makest a feast.
" If there should follow a thousand swords to
    carry my bones away,
" Belike the price of a jackal's meal were more
    than a thief could pay.
" They will feed their horse on the standing
    crop, their men on the garnered
    grain.
" The thatch of the byres will serve their fires
    when all the cattle are slain.
" But if thou thinkest the price be fair,—thy
    brethren wait to sup,
" The hound is kin to the jackal-spawn,—howl,
    dog, and call them up !
" And if thou thinkest the price be high, in steer
    and gear and stack,
" Give me my father's mare again, and I'll fight
    my own way back ! "
Kamal has gripped him by the hand and set him
    upon his feet.
" No talk shall be of dogs," said he, " when wolf
    and grey wolf meet.
" May I eat dirt if thou hast hurt of me in deed or
    breath ;
" What dam of lances brought thee forth to jest
    at the dawn with Death ? "
Lightly answered the Colonel's son : " I hold by
    the blood of my clan :

" Take up the mare for my father's gift—by God,
    she has carried a man ! "
The red mare ran to the Colonel's son, and nuzzled
    against his breast ;
" We be two strong men," said Kamal then, " but
    she loveth the younger best.
" So she shall go with a lifter's dower, my turquoise-
    studded rein,
" My 'broidered saddle and saddle-cloth, and silver
    stirrups twain."
The Colonel's son a pistol drew, and held it
    muzzle-end,
" Ye have taken the one from a foe," said
    he. " Will ye take the mate from a
    friend ? "
" A gift for a gift," said Kamal straight ; " a limb
    for the risk of a limb.
" Thy father has sent his son to me, I'll send my
    son to him ! "
With that he whistled his only son, that dropped
    from a mountain-crest—
He trod the ling like a buck in spring, and he
    looked like a lance in rest.
" Now here is thy master," Kamal said, " who
    leads a troop of the Guides,
" And thou must ride at his left side as shield on
    shoulder rides.
" Till Death or I cut loose the tie, at camp and
    board and bed,
" Thy life is his—thy fate it is to guard him with
    thy head.

" So, thou must eat the White Queen's meat, and
     all her foes are thine,
" And thou must harry thy father's hold for the
     peace of the Border-line.
" And thou must make a trooper tough and hack
     thy way to power—
" Belike they will raise thee to Ressaldar when I
     am hanged in Peshawur ! "

They have looked each other between the eyes,
     and there they found no fault.
They have taken the Oath of the Brother-in-Blood
     on leavened bread and salt :
They have taken the Oath of the Brother-in-Blood
     on fire and fresh-cut sod,
On the hilt and the haft of the Khyber knife, and
     the Wondrous Names of God.
The Colonel's son he rides the mare and Kamal's
     boy the dun,
And two have come back to Fort Bukloh where
     there went forth but one.
And when they drew to the Quarter-Guard, full
     twenty swords flew clear—
There was not a man but carried his feud with the
     blood of the mountaineer.
" Ha' done ! ha' done ! " said the Colonel's son.
     " Put up the steel at your sides !
" Last night ye had struck at a Border thief—
     to-night 'tis a man of the Guides ! "

Oh, East is East, and West is West, and never the
     twain shall meet,

*Till Earth and Sky stand presently at God's great
    Judgment Seat ;*
*But there is neither East nor West, Border, nor Breed,
    nor Birth,*
*When two strong men stand face to face, though they
    come from the ends of the earth !*

"BACK TO THE ARMY AGAIN"

I'M 'ERE in a ticky ulster an' a broken billycock 'at,
A-layin' on to the sergeant I don't know a gun
    from a bat ;
My shirt's doin' duty for jacket, my sock's stickin'
    out o' my boots,
An' I'm learnin' the damned old goose-step along
    o' the new recruits !

    Back to the Army again, sergeant,
      Back to the Army again.
    Don't look so 'ard, for I 'aven't no card,
      I'm back to the Army again !

I done my six years' service. 'Er Majesty sez :
    " Good day—
You'll please to come when you're rung for, an'
    'ere's your 'ole back-pay ;
An' fourpence a day for baccy—an' bloomin'
    gen'rous, too ;
An' now you can make your fortune—the same as
    your orf'cers do."

Back to the Army again, sergeant,
　　Back to the Army again.
'Ow did I learn to do right-about-turn?
　　I'm back to the Army again!

A man of four-an'-twenty that 'asn't learned of a
　　trade—
Beside " Reserve " agin' him—'e'd better be never
　　made.
I tried my luck for a quarter, an' that was enough
　　for me,
An' I thought of 'Er Majesty's barricks, an' I
　　thought I'd go an' see.

Back to the Army again, sergeant,
　　Back to the Army again.
'Tisn't my fault if I dress when I 'alt—
　　I'm back to the Army again!

The sergeant arst no questions, but 'e winked the
　　other eye,
'E sez to me, " 'Shun ! " an' I shunted, the same
　　as in days gone by ;
For 'e saw the set o' my shoulders, an' I couldn't
　　'elp 'oldin' straight
When me an' the other rookies come under the
　　barrick-gate.

Back to the Army again, sergeant,
　　Back to the Army again.
'Oo would ha' thought I could carry an'
　　port?[1]
　　I'm back to the Army again!

[1] Carry and port his rifle.

I took my bath, an' I wallered—for, Gawd, I
    needed it so !
I smelt the smell o' the barricks, I 'eard the bugles
    go.
I 'eard the feet on the gravel—the feet o' the men
    what drill—
An' I sez to my flutterin' 'eart-strings, I sez to 'em,
    " Peace, be still ! "

> Back to the Army again, sergeant,
>   Back to the Army again.
> 'Oo said I knew when the troopship was
>   due ?
> I'm back to the Army again !

I carried my slops to the tailor ; I sez to 'im, " None
    o' your lip !
You tight 'em over the shoulders, an' loose 'em
    over the 'ip,
For the set o' the tunic's 'orrid." An' 'e sez to
    me, " Strike me dead,
But I thought you was used to the business ! "
    an' so 'e done what I said.

> Back to the Army again, sergeant,
>   Back to the Army again.
> Rather too free with my fancies ? Wot—me ?
> I'm back to the Army again !

Next week I'll 'ave 'em fitted ; I'll buy me a
    swagger-cane ;
They'll let me free o' the barricks to walk on the
    Hoe again,

In the name o' William Parsons, that used to be
    Edward Clay,
An'—any pore beggar that wants it can draw my
    fourpence a day !

        Back to the Army again, sergeant,
           Back to the Army again.
        Out o' the cold an' the rain, sergeant,
           Out o' the cold an' the rain.
                        'Oo's there ?

A man's that too good to be lost you,
    A man that is 'andled an' made—
A man that will pay what 'e cost you
    In learnin' the others their trade—parade
You're droppin' the pick o' the Army
    Because you don't 'elp 'em remain,
But drives 'em to cheat to get out o' the street
    An' back to the Army again !

THE MOTHER-LODGE

    THERE was Rundle, Station Master,
        An' Beazeley of the Rail,
    An' 'Ackman, Commissariat,
        An' Donkin' o' the Jail ;
    An' Blake, Conductor-Sergeant,
        Our Master twice was 'e,
    With 'im that kept the Europe-shop,
        Old Framjee Eduljee.

Outside—" Sergeant ! Sir ! Salute ! Salaam ! "
Inside—" Brother," an' it doesn't do no 'arm.

We met upon the Level an' we parted on the Square,
An' I was Junior Deacon in my Mother-Lodge out
there !

We'd Bola Nath, Accountant,
  An' Saul the Aden Jew,
An' Din Mohammed, draughtsman
  Of the Survey Office too ;
There was Babu Chuckerbutty,
  An' Amir Singh the Sikh,
An' Castro from the fittin'-sheds,
  The Roman Catholick !

We 'adn't good regalia,
  An' our Lodge was old an' bare,
But we knew the Ancient Landmarks,
  An' we kep' 'em to a hair ;
An' lookin' on it backwards
  It often strikes me thus,
There ain't such things as infidels,
  Excep', per'aps, it's us.

For monthly, after Labour,
  We'd all sit down and smoke
(We dursn't give no banquets,
  Lest a Brother's caste were broke),
An' man on man got talkin'
  Religion an' the rest,
An' every man comparin'
  Of the God 'e knew the best.

So man on man got talkin',
  An' not a Brother stirred

Till mornin' waked the parrots
    An' that dam' brain-fever-bird;
We'd say 'twas 'ighly curious,
    An' we'd all ride 'ome to bed,
With Mo'ammed, God, an' Shiva
    Changin' pickets in our 'ead.

Full oft on Guv'ment service
    This rovin' foot 'ath pressed,
An' bore fraternal greetin's
    To the Lodges east an' west,
Accordin' as commanded.
    From Kohat to Singapore,
But I wish that I might see them
    In my Mother-Lodge once more!

I wish that I might see them,
    My Brethren black an' brown,
With the trichies smellin' pleasant
    An' the *hog-darn*[1] passin' down;
An' the old khansamah[2] snorin'
    On the bottle-khana[3] floor,
Like a Master in good standing
    With my Mother-Lodge once more.

Outside—" Sergeant! Sir! Salute! Salaam!"
Inside—" Brother," an' it doesn't do no 'arm.
We met upon the Level an' we parted on the Square,
An' I was Junior Deacon in my Mother-Lodge out
    there!

[1] Cigar-lighter.   [2] Butler.   [3] Pantry.

POSSIBILITIES

AY, LAY him 'neath the Simla pine—
  A fortnight fully to be missed,
  Behold, we lose our fourth at whist,
A chair is vacant where we dine.

His place forgets him; other men
  Have bought his ponies, guns, and traps.
  His fortune is the Great Perhaps
And that cool rest-house down the glen,

Whence he shall hear, as spirits may,
  Our mundane revel on the height,
  Shall watch each flashing 'rickshaw-light
Sweep on to dinner, dance, and play.

Benmore shall woo him to the ball
  With lighted rooms and braying band;
  And he shall hear and understand
" Dream Faces " better than us all.

For, think you, as the vapours flee
  Across Sanjaolie after rain,
  His soul may climb the hill again
To each old field of victory.

Unseen, whom women held so dear,
  The strong man's yearning to his kind
  Shall shake at most the window-blind,
Or dull awhile the card-room's cheer.

In his own place of power unknown,
　　His Light o' Love another's flame,
　　His dearest pony galloped lame,
And he an alien and alone !

Yet may he meet with many a friend—
　　Shrewd shadows, lingering long unseen
　　Among us when " *God Save the Queen* "
Shows even " extras " have an end.

And, when we leave the heated room,
　　And, when at four the lights expire,
　　The crew shall gather round the fire
And mock our laughter in the gloom ;

Talk as we talked, and they ere death—
　　Flirt wanly, dance in ghostly-wise,
　　With ghosts of tunes for melodies,
And vanish at the morning's breath !

IF——

IF YOU can keep your head when all about you
　　Are losing theirs and blaming it on you,
If you can trust yourself when all men doubt you,
　　But make allowance for their doubting too ;
If you can wait and not be tired by waiting,
　　Or being lied about, don't deal in lies,
Or being hated don't give way to hating,
　　And yet don't look too good, nor talk too wise :

If you can dream—and not make dreams your
    master ;
    If you can think and not make thoughts your
        aim ;
If you can meet with Triumph and Disaster
    And treat those two impostors just the same ;
If you can bear to hear the truth you've spoken
    Twisted by knaves to make a trap for fools,
Or watch the things you gave your life to, broken,
    And stoop and build 'em up with worn-out
        tools :

If you can make one heap of all your winnings
    And risk it on one turn of pitch-and-toss,
And lose, and start again at your beginnings
    And never breathe a word about your loss ;
If you can force your heart and nerve and sinew
    To serve your turn long after they are gone,
And so hold on when there is nothing in you
    Except the Will which says to them : " Hold
        on ! "

If you can talk with crowds and keep your virtue,
    Or walk with Kings—nor lose the common
        touch,
If neither foes nor loving friends can hurt you,
    If all men count with you, but none too much ;
If you can fill the unforgiving minute
    With sixty seconds' worth of distance run,
Yours is the Earth and everything that's in it,
    And—which is more—you'll be a Man, my son !

ANIMALS

The Law of the Jungle

The Song of the Little Hunter

Road-Song of the *Bandar-Log*

Chapter Headings; Just-So Stories

Four-Feet

" His Apologies "

THE LAW OF THE JUNGLE

*NOW this is the Law of the Jungle—as old and as
    true as the sky;*
*And the Wolf that shall keep it may prosper, but the
    Wolf that shall break it must die.*

*As the creeper that girdles the tree-trunk the Law
    runneth forward and back—*
*For the strength of the Pack is the Wolf, and the
    strength of the Wolf is the Pack.*

Wash daily from nose-tip to tail-tip; drink deeply,
    but never too deep;
And remember the night is for hunting, and forget
    not the day is for sleep.

The Jackal may follow the Tiger, but, Cub, when
    thy whiskers are grown,
Remember the Wolf is a hunter—go forth and get
    food of thine own.

Keep peace with the Lords of the Jungle—the
    Tiger, the Panther, the Bear;
And trouble not Hathi the Silent, and mock not
    the Boar in his lair.

When Pack meets with Pack in the Jungle, and
    neither will go from the trail,

Lie down till the leaders have spoken—it may be
fair words shall prevail.

When ye fight with a Wolf of the Pack, ye must
fight him alone and afar,
Lest others take part in the quarrel, and the Pack
be diminished by war.

The Lair of the Wolf is his refuge, and where he
has made him his home,
Not even the Head Wolf may enter, not even the
Council may come.

The Lair of the Wolf is his refuge, but where he
has digged it too plain,
The Council shall send him a message, and so he
shall change it again.

If ye kill before midnight, be silent, and wake not
the woods with your bay,
Lest ye frighten the deer from the crops, and the
brothers go empty away.

Ye may kill for yourselves, and your mates, and
your cubs as they need, and ye can ;
But kill not for pleasure of killing, and *seven times
never kill Man !*

If ye plunder his Kill from a weaker, devour not
all in thy pride ;
Pack-Right is the right of the meanest ; so leave
him the head and the hide.

The Kill of the Pack is the meat of the Pack. Ye
    must eat where it lies ;
And no one may carry away of that meat to his
    lair, or he dies.

The Kill of the Wolf is the meat of the Wolf. He
    may do what he will,
But, till he has given permission, the Pack may not
    eat of that Kill.

Cub-Right is the right of the Yearling. From all
    of his Pack he may claim
Full-gorge when the killer has eaten ; and none
    may refuse him the same.

Lair-Right is the right of the Mother. From all
    of her year she may claim
One haunch of each kill for her litter ; and none
    may deny her the same.

Cave-Right is the right of the Father—to hunt by
    himself for his own :
He is freed of all calls to the Pack ; he is judged
    by the Council alone.

Because of his age and his cunning, because of his
    gripe and his paw,
In all that the Law leaveth open, the word of the
    Head Wolf is Law.

*Now these are the Laws of the Jungle, and many and
    mighty are they ;*
*But the head and the hoof of the Law and the haunch
    and the hump is—Obey !*

THE SONG OF THE LITTLE
HUNTER

ERE Mor the Peacock flutters, ere the Monkey
    People cry,
  Ere Chil the Kite swoops down a furlong sheer,
Through the Jungle very softly flits a shadow and
    a sigh—
  He is Fear, O Little Hunter, he is Fear !
Very softly down the glade runs a waiting,
    watching shade,
  And the whisper spreads and widens far and near.
And the sweat is on thy brow, for he passes even
    now—
  He is Fear, O Little Hunter, he is Fear !

Ere the moon has climbed the mountain, ere the
    rocks are ribbed with light,
  When the downward-dipping trails are dank
    and drear,

Comes a breathing hard behind thee—*snuffle-
    snuffle* through the night—
  It is Fear, O Little Hunter, it is Fear !
On thy knees and draw the bow ; bid the shrilling
    arrow go ;
  In the empty, mocking thicket plunge the spear !
But thy hands are loosed and weak, and the blood
    has left thy cheek —
  It is Fear, O Little Hunter, it is Fear !

When the heat-cloud sucks the tempest, when the
    slivered pine-trees fall,
  When the blinding, blaring rain-squalls lash and
    veer,
Through the war-gongs of the thunder rings a
    voice more loud than all—
  It is Fear, O Little Hunter, it is Fear !
Now the spates are banked and deep ; now the
    footless boulders leap—
  Now the lightning shows each littlest leaf-rib
    clear—
But thy throat is shut and dried, and thy heart
    against thy side
  Hammers : Fear, O Little Hunter—this is Fear !

ROAD-SONG OF THE *BANDAR-LOG*

HERE we go in a flung festoon,
Half-way up to the jealous moon !
Don't you envy our pranceful bands ?
Don't you wish you had extra hands ?
Wouldn't you like if your tails were—*so*—
Curved in the shape of a Cupid's bow ?
    Now you're angry, but—never mind,
    Brother, thy tail hangs down behind !

Here we sit in a branchy row,
Thinking of beautiful things we know ;
Dreaming of deeds that we mean to do,
All complete, in a minute or two—
Something noble and grand and good,
Won by merely wishing we could.
    Now we're going to—never mind,
    Brother, thy tail hangs down behind !

All the talk we ever have heard
Uttered by bat or beast or bird—
Hide or fin or scale or feather—
Jabber it quickly and all together !
Excellent !   Wonderful !   Once again !
Now we are talking just like men.
    Let's pretend we are . . . Never mind !
    Brother, thy tail hangs down behind !
    This is the way of the Monkey-kind !

Then join our leaping lines that scumfish through the pines,
That rocket by where, light and high, the wild-grape swings.
By the rubbish in our wake, and the noble noise we make,
Be sure—be sure, we're going to do some splendid things !

CHAPTER HEADINGS

JUST-SO STORIES

WHEN the cabin port-holes are dark and green
  Because of the seas outside ;
When the ship goes *wop* (with a wiggle between)
And the steward falls into the soup-tureen,
  And the trunks begin to slide ;
When Nursey lies on the floor in a heap,
And Mummy tells you to let her sleep,
And you aren't waked or washed or dressed,
Why, then you will know (if you haven't guessed)
You're " Fifty North and Forty West ! "

How the Whale Got His Throat.

The Camel's hump is an ugly lump
  Which well you may see at the Zoo ;
But uglier yet is the hump we get
  From having too little to do.

Kiddies and grown-ups too-oo-oo,
If we haven't enough to do-oo-oo,
                    We get the hump—
                    Cameelious hump—
The hump that is black and blue !

We climb out of bed with a frouzly head,
    And a snarly-yarly voice.
We shiver and scowl and we grunt and we growl
    At our bath and our boots and our toys ;

And there ought to be a corner for me
(And I know there is one for you)
                    When we get the hump—
                    Cameelious hump—
The hump that is black and blue !

The cure for this ill is not to sit still,
    Or frowst with a book by the fire ;
But to take a large hoe and a shovel also,
    And dig till you gently perspire ;

And then you will find that the sun and the wind,
And the Djinn of the Garden too,
                    Have lifted the hump—
                    The horrible hump—
The hump that is black and blue !

I get it as well as you-oo-oo—
If I haven't enough to do-oo-oo !
We all get hump—
Cameelious hump—
Kiddies and grown-ups too !

How the Camel Got His Hump.

I am the Most Wise Baviaan, saying in most wise
   tones,
" Let us melt into the landscape—just us two by
   our lones."
People have come—in a carriage—calling. But
   Mummy is there. . . .
Yes, I can go if you take me—Nurse says *she* don't
   care.
Let's go up to the pig-styes and sit on the farmyard
   rails !
Let's say things to the bunnies, and watch 'em
   skitter their tails !
Let's—oh, *anything*, daddy, so long as it's you and
   me,
And going truly exploring, and not being in till
   tea !
Here's your boots (I've brought 'em), and here's
   your cap and stick,
And here's your pipe and tobacco. Oh, come
   along out of it—quick !

How the Leopard Got His Spots.

I keep six honest serving-men
   (They taught me all I knew);
Their names are What and Why and When
   And How and Where and Who.
I send them over land and sea,
   I send them east and west;
But after they have worked for me,
   I give them all a rest.

I let them rest from nine till five,
   For I am busy then,
As well as breakfast, lunch, and tea,
   For they are hungry men.
But different folk have different views.
   I know a person small—
She keeps ten million serving-men,
   Who get no rest at all !

She sends 'em abroad on her own affairs,
   From the second she opens her eyes—
One million Hows, two million Wheres,
   And seven million Whys !

                      The Elephant's Child.

This is the mouth-filling song of the race that was
   run by a Boomer.
Run in a single burst—only event of its kind—
Started by Big God Nqong from Warrigaborri-
   garooma,
Old Man Kangaroo first, Yellow-Dog Dingo
   behind.

Kangaroo bounded away, his back-legs working
   like pistons—
Bounded from morning till dark, twenty-five feet
   at a bound.
Yellow-Dog Dingo lay like a yellow cloud in the
   distance—
Much too busy to bark. My! but they covered
   the ground!

Nobody knows where they went, or followed the
   track that they flew in,
For that Continent hadn't been given a name.
They ran thirty degrees, from Torres Straits to the
   Leeuwin
(Look at the Atlas, please), then they ran back
   as they came.

S'posing you could trot from Adelaide to the
   Pacific,
For an afternoon's run—half what these gentlemen
   did—

You would feel rather hot, but your legs would
    develop terrific—
Yes, my importunate son, you'd be a Marvellous
    Kid !
        The Sing-Song of Old Man Kangaroo.

I've never sailed the Amazon,
   I've never reached Brazil ;
But the *Don* and *Magdalena*,
   They can go there when they will !

        Yes, weekly from Southampton,
        Great steamers, white and gold,
        Go rolling down to Rio
        (Roll down—roll down to Rio !)
        And I'd like to roll to Rio
        Some day before I'm old !

I've never seen a Jaguar,
   Nor yet an Armadill-
o dilloing in his armour,
   And I s'pose I never will,

        Unless I go to Rio
        These wonders to behold—
        Roll down—roll down to Rio—
        Roll really down to Rio !
        Oh, I'd love to roll to Rio
        Some day before I'm old !
        The Beginning of the Armadilloes.

China-going P. and O.'s
Pass Pau Amma's playground close,
And his Pusat Tasek lies
Near the track of most B.I.'s
N.Y.K. and N.D.L.
Know Pau Amma's home as well
As the Fisher of the Sea knows
" Bens," M.M.'s and Rubattinos.
But (and this is rather queer)
A.T.L.'s can *not* come here ;
O. and O. and D.O.A.
Must go round another way.
Orient, Anchor, Bibby, Hall,
Never go that way at all.
U.C.S. would have a fit
If it found itself on it.
And if " Beavers " took their cargoes
To Penang instead of Lagos,
Or a fat Shaw-Savill bore
Passengers to Singapore,
Or a White Star were to try a
Little trip to Sourabaya,
Or a B.S.A. went on
Past Natal to Cheribon,
Then great Mr. Lloyds would come
With a wire and drag them home !

.   .   .   .   .

You'll know what my riddle means
When you've eaten mangosteens.

The Crab That Played with the Sea.

Pussy can sit by the fire and sing,
    Pussy can climb a tree,
Or play with a silly old cork and string
    To 'muse herself, not me.
But *I* like *Binkie* my dog, because
    He knows how to behave ;
So, *Binkie's* the same as the First Friend was,
    And I am the Man in the Cave !

Pussy will play man-Friday till
    It's time to wet her paw
And make her walk on the window-sill
    (For the footprint Crusoe saw) ;
Then she fluffles her tail and mews,
    And scratches and won't attend.
But *Binkie* will play whatever I choose,
    And he is my true First Friend !

Pussy will rub my knees with her head
    Pretending she loves me hard ;
But the very minute I go to my bed
    Pussy runs out in the yard,
And there she stays till the morning-light ;
    So I know it is only pretend ;
But *Binkie*, he snores at my feet all night,
    And he is my Firstest Friend !

                The Cat That Walked by Himself.

There was never a Queen like Balkis,
   From here to the wide world's end ;
But Balkis talked to a butterfly
   As you would talk to a friend.

There was never a King like Solomon,
   Not since the world began ;
But Solomon talked to a butterfly
   As a man would talk to a man.

She was Queen of Sabæa—
   And *he* was Asia's Lord—
But they both of 'em talked to butterflies
   When they took their walks abroad !

              The Butterfly That Stamped.

FOUR-FEET

I HAVE done mostly what most men do,
   And pushed it out of my mind ;
But I can't forget, if I wanted to,
   Four-Feet trotting behind.

Day after day, the whole day through—
   Wherever my road inclined—
Four-Feet said, " I am coming with you ! "
   And trotted along behind.

Now I must go by some other round,—
Which I shall never find—
Somewhere that does not carry the sound
Of Four-Feet trotting behind.

"HIS APOLOGIES"

1932

MASTER, this is Thy Servant. He is rising eight
   weeks old.
He is mainly Head and Tummy. His legs are
   uncontrolled.
But Thou has forgiven his ugliness, and settled
   him on Thy knee . . .
Art Thou content with Thy Servant? He is *very*
   comfy with Thee.

Master, behold a Sinner! He hath committed a
   wrong.
He hath defiled Thy Premises through being kept
   in too long.
Wherefore his nose has been rubbed in the dirt,
   and his self-respect has been bruisèd,
Master, pardon Thy Sinner, and see he is properly
   loosèd.

Master—again Thy Sinner! This that was once
   Thy Shoe,

He has found and taken and carried aside, as fitting
    matter to chew.
Now there is neither blacking nor tongue, and the
    Housemaid has us in tow.
Master, remember Thy Servant is young, and tell
    her to let him go !

Master, extol Thy Servant, he has met a most
    Worthy Foe !
There has been fighting all over the Shop—and
    into the Shop also !
Till cruel umbrellas parted the strife (or I might
    have been choking him yet)
But Thy Servant has had the Time of his Life—
    and now shall we call on the vet ?

Master, behold Thy Servant ! Strange children
    came to play,
And because they fought to caress him, Thy
    Servant wentedst away.
But now that the Little Beasts have gone, he has
    returned to see
(Brushed—with his Sunday collar on) what they
    left over from tea.

.   .   .   .   .

Master, pity Thy Servant ! He is deaf and three
    parts blind.
He cannot catch Thy Commandments. He cannot
    read Thy Mind.

Oh, leave him not to his loneliness ; nor make
   him that kitten's scorn.
He hath had none other God than Thee since the
   year that he was born.

Lord, look down on Thy Servant ! Bad things
   have come to pass.
There is no heat in the midday sun, nor health in
   the wayside grass.
His bones are full of an old disease—his torments
   run and increase.
Lord, make haste with Thy Lightnings and grant
   him a quick release !

ADVENTURE

THE SONG OF THE BANJO

1894

You couldn't pack a Broadwood half a mile—
  You mustn't leave a fiddle in the damp—
You couldn't raft an organ up the Nile,
  And play it in an Equatorial swamp.
I travel with the cooking-pots and pails—
  I'm sandwiched 'tween the coffee and the pork—
And when the dusty column checks and tails,
  You should hear me spur the rearguard to a
      walk !

      With my " *Pilly-willy-winky-winky-popp !* "
        (Oh, it's any tune that comes into my head !)
      So I keep 'em moving forward till they drop ;
        So I play 'em up to water and to bed.

In the silence of the camp before the fight,
  When it's good to make your will and say your
      prayer,
You can hear my *strumpty-tumpty* overnight,
  Explaining ten to one was always fair.
I'm the Prophet of the Utterly Absurd,
  Of the Patently Impossible and Vain—
And when the Thing that Couldn't has occurred,
  Give me time to change my leg and go again.

135

With my " *Tumpa-tumpa-tumpa-tumpa-tump !* "
    In the desert where the dung-fed camp-
        smoke curled.
There was never voice before us till I led our
    lonely chorus,
      I—the war-drum of the White Man round
      the world !

By the bitter road the Younger Son must tread,
    Ere he win to hearth and saddle of his own,—
'Mid the riot of the shearers at the shed,
    In the silence of the herder's hut alone—
In the twilight, on a bucket upside down,
    Hear me babble what the weakest won't
      confess—
I am Memory and Torment—I am Town !
    I am all that ever went with evening dress !

    With my " *Tunka-tunka-tunka-tunka-tunk !* "
      (So the lights—the London Lights—grow
      near and plain !)
    So I rowel 'em afresh towards the Devil and
      the Flesh,
      Till I bring my broken rankers home again.

In desire of many marvels over sea,
    Where the new-raised tropic city sweats and
      roars,
I have sailed with Young Ulysses from the quay
    Till the anchor rumbled down on stranger
      shores.

He is blooded to the open and the sky,
  He is taken in a snare that shall not fail,
He shall hear me singing strongly, till he die,
  Like the shouting of a backstay in a gale.

     With my " *Hya ! Heeya ! Heeya ! Hullah !
         Haul !* "
         (Oh the green that thunders aft along the
             deck !)
     Are you sick o' towns and men ? You must
         sign and sail again,
         For it's " Johnny Bowlegs, pack your kit
             and trek ! "

Through the gorge that gives the stars at noon-
         day clear—
  Up the pass that packs the scud beneath our
         wheel—
Round the bluff that sinks her thousand fathom
         sheer—
  Down the valley with our guttering brakes
         asqueal :
Where the trestle groans and quivers in the snow,
  Where the many-shedded levels loop and twine.
Hear me lead my reckless children from below
  Till we sing the Song of Roland to the pine !

     With my " *Tinka-tinka-tinka-tinka-tink !* "
         (Oh the axe has cleared the mountain,
             croup and crest !)

And we ride the iron stallions down to drink
    Through the cañons to the waters of th
        West !

And the tunes that mean so much to you alone—
    Common tunes that make you choke and blow
        your nose—
Vulgar tunes that bring the laugh that brings th
        groan—
    I can rip your very heartstrings out with those
With the feasting, and the folly, and the fun—
    And the lying, and the lusting, and the drink,
And the merry play that drops you, when you'r
        done,
    To the thoughts that burn like irons if you think

    With my " *Plunka-lunka-lunka-lunka-lunk !* "
        Here's a trifle on account of pleasure past,
    Ere the wit that made you win gives you eye
        to see your sin
        And—the heavier repentance at the last !

Let the organ moan her sorrow to the roof—
    I have told the naked stars the Grief of Man !
Let the trumpet snare the foeman to the proof—
    I have known Defeat, and mocked it as we ran
My bray ye may not alter nor mistake
    When I stand to jeer the fatted Soul of Things,
But the Song of Lost Endeavour that I make,
    Is it hidden in the twanging of the strings ?

With my " *Ta-ra-rara-rara-ra-ra-rrrp !* "
   (Is it naught to you that hear and pass me
      by ?)
But the word—the word is mine, when the
    order moves the line
    And the lean, locked ranks go roaring
      down to die !

he grandam of my grandam was the Lyre—
   (O the blue below the little fisher-huts !)
hat the Stealer stooping beachward filled with
    fire,
   Till she bore my iron head and ringing guts !
y the wisdom of the centuries I speak—
   To the tune of yestermorn I set the truth—
the joy of life unquestioned—I, the Greek—
   I, the everlasting Wonder-song of Youth !

    With my " *Tinka-tinka-tinka-tinka-tink !* "
      (What d'ye lack, my noble masters !   What
        d'ye lack ?)
    So I draw the world together link by link :
      Yea, from Delos up to Limerick and back !

MANDALAY

Y THE old Moulmein Pagoda, lookin' lazy at the
   sea,
here's a Burma girl a-settin', and I know she
   thinks o' me ;

For the wind is in the palm-trees, and the temple
      bells they say :
" Come you back, you British soldier ; come you
      back to Mandalay ! "
          Come you back to Mandalay,
          Where the old Flotilla lay :
          Can't you 'ear their paddles chunkin' from
              Rangoon to Mandalay ?
          On the road to Mandalay,
          Where the flyin'-fishes play,
          An' the dawn comes up like thunder outer
              China 'crost the Bay !

'Er petticoat was yaller an' 'er little cap was green,
An' 'er name was Supi-yaw-lat—jes' the same as
      Theebaw's Queen,
An' I seed her first a-smokin' of a whackin' white
      cheroot,
An' a-wastin' Christian kisses on an 'eathen idol's
      foot :
          Bloomin' idol made o' mud—
          Wot they called the Great Gawd Budd—
          Plucky lot she cared for idols when I kissed
             'er where she stud !
          On the road to Mandalay . . .

When the mist was on the rice-fields an' the sun
      was droppin' slow,
She'd git 'er little banjo an' she'd sing " *Kulla-
lo-lo !* "

With 'er arm upon my shoulder an' 'er cheek agin
    my cheek
We useter watch the steamers an' the *hathis* pilin'
    teak.
        Elephints a-pilin' teak
        In the sludgy, squdgy creek,
        Where the silence 'ung that 'eavy you was
            'arf afraid to speak !
        On the road to Mandalay . . .

But that's all shove be'ind me—long ago an' fur
    away,
An' there ain't no 'busses runnin' from the Bank
    to Mandalay ;
An' I'm learnin' 'ere in London what the ten-year
    soldier tells :
" If you've 'eard the East a-callin', you won't
    never 'eed naught else."
        No ! you won't 'eed nothin' else
        But them spicy garlic smells,
        An' the sunshine an' the palm-trees an' the
            tinkly temple-bells ;
        On the road to Mandalay . . .

I am sick o' wastin' leather on these gritty pavin'-
    stones,
An' the blasted English drizzle wakes the fever in
    my bones ;
Tho' I walks with fifty 'ousemaids outer Chelsea
    to the Strand,

An' they talks a lot o' lovin', but wot do they
    understand ?
        Beefy face an' grubby 'and—
        Law ! wot do they understand ?
        I've a neater, sweeter maiden in a cleaner
           greener land !
        On the road to Mandalay . . .

Ship me somewheres east of Suez, where the best
    is like the worst,
Where there aren't no Ten Commandments an' a
    man can raise a thirst ;
For the temple-bells are callin', an' it's there that
    I would be—
By the old Moulmein Pagoda, looking lazy at the
    sea ;
        On the road to Mandalay,
        Where the old Flotilla lay,
        With our sick beneath the awnings when
           we went to Mandalay !
        O the road to Mandalay,
        Where the flyin'-fishes play,
        An' the dawn comes up like thunder outer
           China 'crost the Bay !

THE PRODIGAL SON

(WESTERN VERSION)

HERE come I to my own again,
Fed, forgiven and known again,
Claimed by bone of my bone again
And cheered by flesh of my flesh.
The fatted calf is dressed for me,
But the husks have greater zest for me,
I think my pigs will be best for me,
So I'm off to the Yards afresh.

I never was very refined, you see,
(And it weighs on my brother's mind, you see)
But there's no reproach among swine, d'you see,
For being a bit of a swine.
So I'm off with wallet and staff to eat
The bread that is three parts chaff to wheat,
But glory be !—there's a laugh to it,
Which isn't the case when we dine.

My father glooms and advises me,
My brother sulks and despises me,
And Mother catechises me
Till I want to go out and swear.
And, in spite of the butler's gravity,
I know that the servants have it I
Am a monster of moral depravity,
And I'm damned if I think it's fair !

I wasted my substance, I know I did,
On riotous living, so I did,
But there's nothing on record to show I did
More than my betters have done.
They talk of the money I spent out there—
They hint at the pace that I went out there—
But they all forget I was sent out there
Alone as a rich man's son.

So I was a mark for plunder at once,
And lost my cash (can you wonder?) at once,
But I didn't give up and knock under at once.
I worked in the Yards, for a spell,
Where I spent my nights and my days with hogs,
And shared their milk and maize with hogs,
Till, I guess, I have learned what pays with hogs
And—I have that knowledge to sell!

So back I go to my job again,
Not so easy to rob again,
Or quite so ready to sob again
On any neck that's around.
I'm leaving, Pater. Good-bye to you!
God bless you, Mater! I'll write to you . . .
I wouldn't be impolite to you,
But, Brother, you *are* a hound!

THE LOST LEGION

1895

THERE's a Legion that never was 'listed,
    That carries no colours or crest.
But, split in a thousand detachments,
    Is breaking the road for the rest.
Our fathers they left us their blessing—
    They taught us, and groomed us, and crammed;
But we've shaken the Clubs and the Messes
    To go and find out and be damned
                    (Dear boys !),
    To go and get shot and be damned.

So some of us chivvy the slaver,
    And some of us cherish the black,
And some of us hunt on the Oil Coast,
    And some on the Wallaby track :
And some of us drift to Sarawak,
    And some of us drift up The Fly,
And some share our tucker with tigers,
    And some with the gentle Masai,
                    (Dear boys !),
    Take tea with the giddy Masai.

We've painted The Islands vermilion,
    We've pearled on half-shares in the Bay,

We've shouted on seven-ounce nuggets,
    We've starved on a Seedeeboy's pay ;
We've laughed at the world as we found it,—
    Its women and cities and men—
From Sayyid Burgash in a tantrum
    To the smoke-reddened eyes of Loben,
                        (Dear boys !),
    We've a little account with Loben.

The ends of the Earth were our portion,
    The ocean at large was our share.
There was never a skirmish to windward
    But the Leaderless Legion was there :
Yes, somehow and somewhere and always
    We were first when the trouble began,
From a lottery-row in Manila,
    To an I.D.B. race on the Pan
                        (Dear boys !),
    With the Mounted Police on the Pan.

We preach in advance of the Army,
    We skirmish ahead of the Church,
With never a gunboat to help us
    When we're scuppered and left in the lurch.
But we know as the cartridges finish,
    And we're filed on our last little shelves,
That the Legion that never was 'listed
    Will send us as good as ourselves
                        (Good men !),
    Five hundred as good as ourselves !

Then a health (we must drink it in whispers),
    To our wholly unauthorized horde—
To the line of our dusty foreloopers,
    The Gentlemen Rovers abroad—
Yes, a health to ourselves ere we scatter,
    For the steamer won't wait for the train,
And the Legion that never was 'listed
    Goes back into quarters again!
                            'Regards!
    Goes back under canvas again.
                            Hurrah!
    The swag and the billy again.
                            Here's how!
    The trail and the packhorse again.
                            Salue!
    The trek and the lager again!

THE EXPLORER

1898

"THERE's no sense in going further—it's the edge
        of cultivation,"
    So they said, and I believed it—broke my land
        and sowed my crop—
Built my barns and strung my fences in the little
        border station
    Tucked away below the foothills where the trails
        run out and stop:

Till a voice, as bad as Conscience, rang inter-
    minable changes
  On one everlasting Whisper day and night
    repeated—so :
"Something hidden. Go and find it. Go and
    look behind the Ranges—
  "Something lost behind the Ranges. Lost and
    waiting for you. Go ! "

So I went, worn out of patience ; never told my
    nearest neighbours—
  Stole away with pack and ponies—left 'em
    drinking in the town ;
And the faith that moveth mountains didn't seem
    to help my labours
  As I faced the sheer main-ranges, whipping up
    and leading down.

March by march I puzzled through 'em, turning
    flanks and dodging shoulders,
  Hurried on in hope of water, headed back for
    lack of grass ;
Till I camped above the tree-line—drifted snow
    and naked boulders—
  Felt free air astir to windward—knew I'd
    stumbled on the Pass.

'Thought to name it for the finder : but that night
    the Norther found me—
  Froze and killed the plains-bred ponies ; so I
    called the camp Despair

It's the Railway Gap to-day, though).   Then my
        Whisper waked to hound me :—
  " Something lost behind the Ranges.   Over
        yonder !   Go you there ! "

Then I knew, the while I doubted—knew His
        Hand was certain o'er me.
  Still—it might be self-delusion—scores of better
       men had died—
I could reach the township living, but . . . He
        knows what terror tore me . . .
  But I didn't . . . but I didn't.   I went down
       the other side,

Till the snow ran out in flowers, and the flowers
        turned to aloes,
  And the aloes sprung to thickets and a brimming
       stream ran by ;
But the thickets dwined to thorn-scrub, and the
        water drained to shallows,
  And I dropped again on desert—blasted earth,
       and blasting sky. . . .

I remember lighting fires ;   I remember sitting by
        'em ;
  I remember seeing faces, hearing voices, through
       the smoke ;
I remember they were fancy—for I threw a stone
        to try 'em.
  " Something lost behind the Ranges " was the
       only word they spoke.

I remember going crazy. I remember that
    knew it
  When I heard myself hallooing to the funn
    folk I saw.
'Very full of dreams that desert, but my two leg
    took me through it . . .
  And I used to watch 'em moving with the toe
    all black and raw.

But at last the country altered—White Man'
    country past disputing—
  Rolling grass and open timber, with a hint o
    hills behind—
There I found me food and water, and I lay a weel
    recruiting.
  Got my strength and lost my nightmares. Ther
    I entered on my find.

Thence I ran my first rough survey—chose m
    trees and blazed and ringed 'em—
  Week by week I pried and sampled—week by
    week my findings grew.
Saul he went to look for donkeys, and by God he
    found a kingdom!
  But by God, who sent His Whisper, I had
    struck the worth of two!

Up along the hostile mountains, where the hair-
    poised snow-slide shivers—
  Down and through the big fat marshes that the
    virgin ore-bed stains,

Till I heard the mile-wide mutterings of un-
    imagined rivers,
  And beyond the nameless timber saw illimitable
    plains !

'Plotted sites of future cities, traced the easy grades
    between 'em ;
  Watched unharnessed rapids wasting fifty
    thousand head an hour ;
Counted leagues of water-frontage through the
    axe-ripe woods that screen 'em—
  Saw the plant to feed a people—up and waiting
    for the power !

Well I know who'll take the credit—all the clever
    chaps that followed—
  Came, a dozen men together—never knew my
    desert-fears ;
Tracked me by the camps I'd quitted, used the
    water-holes I'd hollowed.
  They'll go back and do the talking. *They'll* be
    called the Pioneers !

They will find my sites of townships—not the
    cities that I set there.
  They will rediscover rivers—not my rivers
    heard at night.
By my own old marks and bearings they will show
    me how to get there,
  By the lonely cairns I builded they will guide
    my feet aright.

Have I named one single river? Have I claimed
    one single acre?
  Have I kept one single nugget—(barring
    samples)? No, not I!
Because my price was paid me ten times over by
    my Maker.
  But you wouldn't understand it. You go up
    and occupy.

Ores you'll find there; wood and cattle; water-
    transit sure and steady
  (That should keep the railway-rates down), coal
    and iron at your doors.
God took care to hide that country till He judged
    His people ready,
  Then He chose me for His Whisper, and I've
    found it, and it's yours!

Yes, your "Never-never country"—yes, your
    "edge of cultivation"
  And "no sense in going further"—till I crossed
    the range to see.
God forgive me! No, I didn't. It's God's
    present to our nation.
  Anybody might have found it but—His Whisper
    came to Me!

CITIES AND THRONES AND POWERS

THE FOUR ANGELS

As ADAM lay a-dreaming beneath the Apple Tree
The Angel of the Earth came down, and offered
Earth in fee ;
But Adam did not need it,
Nor the plough he would not speed it,
Singing :—" Earth and Water, Air and Fire,
What more can mortal man desire ? "
(The Apple Tree's in bud.)

As Adam lay a-dreaming beneath the Apple Tree
The Angel of the Waters offered all the Seas in fee ;
But Adam would not take 'em,
Nor the ships he wouldn't make 'em,
Singing :—" Water, Earth and Air and Fire,
What more can mortal man desire ? "
(The Apple Tree's in leaf.)

As Adam lay a-dreaming beneath the Apple Tree
The Angel of the Air he offered all the Air in fee ;
But Adam did not crave it,
Nor the flight he wouldn't brave it,
Singing —" Air and Water, Earth and Fire,
What more can mortal man desire ? "
(The Apple Tree's in bloom.)

As Adam lay a-dreaming beneath the Apple-Tree,
The Angel of the Fire rose up and not a word
said he ;
But he wished a flame and made it,
And in Adam's heart he laid it,

Singing :—" Fire, Fire, burning Fire !
        Stand up and reach your heart's desire ! "
            (The Apple Blossom's set.)

As Adam was a-working outside of Eden-Wall,
He used the Earth, he used the Seas, he used the
    Air and all ;
        Till out of black disaster
        He arose to be the master
            Of Earth and Water, Air and Fire,
            But never reached his heart's desire !
                (The Apple Tree's cut down !)

THE CONUNDRUM OF THE WORKSHOPS

1890

WHEN the flush of a new-born sun fell first on
    Eden's green and gold,
Our father Adam sat under the Tree and scratched
    with a stick in the mould ;
And the first rude sketch that the world had seen
    was joy to his mighty heart,
Till the Devil whispered behind the leaves, " It's
    pretty, but is it Art ? "

Wherefore he called to his wife, and fled to fashion
    his work anew—
The first of his race who cared a fig for the first,
    most dread review ;
And he left his lore to the use of his sons—and
    that was a glorious gain

When the Devil chuckled " Is it Art ? " in the ear
    of the branded Cain.

They builded a tower to shiver the sky and wrench
    the stars apart,
Till the Devil grunted behind the bricks : " It's
    striking, but is it Art ? "
The stone was dropped at the quarry-side and the
    idle derrick swung,
While each man talked of the aims of Art, and each
    in an alien tongue.

They fought and they talked in the North and the
    South ; they talked and they fought in the
    West,
Till the waters rose on the pitiful land, and the
    poor Red Clay had rest—
Had rest till that dank blank-canvas dawn when
    the Dove was preened to start,
And the Devil bubbled below the keel : " It's
    human, but is it Art ? "

The tale is as old as the Eden Tree—and new as
    the new-cut tooth—
For each man knows ere his lip-thatch grows he
    is master of Art and Truth ;
And each man hears as the twilight nears, to the
    beat of his dying heart,
The Devil drum on the darkened pane : " You
    did it, but was it Art ? "

We have learned to whittle the Eden Tree to the
    shape of a surplice-peg,

We have learned to bottle our parents twain in the
    yelk of an addled egg,
We know that the tail must wag the dog, for the
    horse is drawn by the cart;
But the Devil whoops, as he whooped of old:
    " It's clever, but is it Art ? "

When the flicker of London sun falls faint on the
    Club-room's green and gold,
The sons of Adam sit them down and scratch with
    their pens in the mould—
They scratch with their pens in the mould of their
    graves, and the ink and the anguish start,
For the Devil mutters behind the leaves : " It's
    pretty, but is it Art ? "

Now, if we could win to the Eden Tree where the
    Four Great Rivers flow,
And the Wreath of Eve is red on the turf as she
    left it long ago,
And if we could come when the sentry slept and
    softly scurry through,
By the favour of God we might know as much—
    as our father Adam knew !

THE PRESS

THE Soldier may forget his Sword,
    The Sailorman the Sea,
The Mason may forget the Word
    And the Priest his Litany :
The Maid may forget both jewel and gem,
    And the Bride her wedding-dress—

But the Jew shall forget Jerusalem
  Ere we forget the Press !

Who once hath stood through the loaded hour
  Ere, roaring like the gale,
The Harrild and the Hoe devour
  Their league-long paper-bale,
And has lit his pipe in the morning calm
  That follows the midnight stress—
He hath sold his heart to the old Black Art
  We call the daily Press.

Who once hath dealt in the widest game
  That all of a man can play,
No later love, no larger fame
  Will lure him long away.
As the war-horse snuffeth the battle afar,
  The entered Soul, no less,
He saith : " Ha ! Ha ! " where the trumpets are
  And the thunders of the Press !

Canst thou number the days that we fulfil,
  Or the *Times* that we bring forth ?
Canst thou send the lightnings to do thy will,
  And cause them reign on earth ?
Hast thou given a peacock goodly wings,
  To please his foolishness ?
Sit down at the heart of men and things,
  Companion of the Press !

The Pope may launch his Interdict,
  The Union its decree,
But the bubble is blown and the bubble is pricked
  By Us and such as We.

Remember the battle and stand aside
　　While Thrones and Powers confess
That King over all the children of pride
　　Is the Press—the Press—the Press !

THE KING

1894

" FAREWELL, Romance ! " the Cave-men said ;
　　" With bone well carved he went away.
" Flint arms the ignoble arrowhead,
　　" And jasper tips the spear to-day.
" Changed are the Gods of Hunt and Dance,
" And He with these.　Farewell, Romance ! "

" Farewell, Romance ! " the Lake-folk sighed ;
　　" We lift the weight of flatling years ;
" The caverns of the mountain-side
　　" Hold Him who scorns our hutted piers.
" Lost hills whereby we dare not dwell,
" Guard ye His rest.　Romance, Farewell ! "

" Farewell, Romance ! " the Soldier spoke ;
　　" By sleight of sword we may not win,
" But scuffle 'mid uncleanly smoke
　　" Of arquebus and culverin.
" Honour is lost, and none may tell
" Who paid good blows.　Romance, farewell ! "

" Farewell, Romance ! " the Traders cried ;
　　" Our keels have lain with every sea.

" The dull-returning wind and tide
    " Heave up the wharf where we would be ;
" The known and noted breezes swell
" Our trudging sails.   Romance, farewell ! "

" Good-bye, Romance ! " the Skipper said ;
    " He vanished with the coal we burn.
" Our dial marks full-steam ahead,
    " Our speed is timed to half a turn.
" Sure as the ferried barge we ply
" 'Twixt port and port.   Romance, good-bye ! "

" Romance ! " the season-tickets mourn,
    " *He* never ran to catch his train,
" But passed with coach and guard and horn—
    " And left the local—late again !
" Confound Romance ! " . . . And all unseen
Romance brought up the nine-fifteen.

His hand was on the lever laid,
    His oil-can soothed the worrying cranks,
His whistle waked the snowbound grade,
    His fog-horn cut the reeking Banks ;
By dock and deep and mine and mill
The Boy-god reckless laboured still !

Robed, crowned and throned, He wove his spell,
    Where heart-blood beat or hearth-smoke
        curled,
With unconsidered miracle,
    Hedged in a backward-gazing world :
Then taught his chosen bard to say :
" Our King was with us—yesterday ! "

COLD IRON

"*GOLD is for the mistress—silver for the maid—*
Copper for the craftsman cunning at his trade."
"Good !" said the Baron, sitting in his hall,
"But Iron—Cold Iron—is master of them all.".

So he made rebellion 'gainst the King his liege,
Camped before his citadel and summoned it to
    siege.
"Nay !" said the cannoneer on the castle wall,
"But Iron—Cold Iron—shall be master of you
    all !"

Woe for the Baron and his knights so strong,
When the cruel cannon-balls laid 'em all along ;
He was taken prisoner, he was cast in thrall,
And Iron—Cold Iron—was master of it all !

Yet his King spake kindly (ah, how kind a Lord !)
"What if I release thee now and give thee back
    thy sword ? "
"Nay !" said the Baron, " mock not at my fall,
For Iron—Cold Iron—is master of men all."

"*Tears are for the craven, prayers are for the clown—*
Halters for the silly neck that cannot keep a crown."
"As my loss is grievous, so my hope is small,
For Iron—Cold Iron—must be master of men all ! "

Yet his King made answer (few such Kings there
    be !)
" Here is Bread and here is Wine—sit and sup with
    me.

Eat and drink in Mary's Name, the whiles I do
    recall
How Iron—Cold Iron—can be master of men all ! "

He took the Wine and blessed it.   He blessed and
    brake the Bread.
With His own Hands He served Them, and
    presently He said :
" See ! These Hands they pierced with nails,
    outside My city wall,
Show Iron—Cold Iron—to be master of men all.

" Wounds are for the desperate, blows are for the
    strong.
Balm and oil for weary hearts all cut and bruised
    with wrong.
I forgive thy treason—I redeem thy fall—
For Iron—Cold Iron—must be master of men all ! "

" *Crowns are for the valiant—sceptres for the bold !*
Thrones and powers for mighty men who dare to take
    and hold ! "
" Nay ! " said the Baron, kneeling in his hall,
" But Iron—Cold Iron—is master of men all !
Iron out of Calvary is master of men all ! "

A SONG OF TRAVEL

WHERE's the lamp that Hero lit
    Once to call Leander home ?
Equal Time hath shovelled it
    'Neath the wrack of Greece and Rome.

Neither wait we any more
That worn sail which Argo bore.

Dust and dust of ashes close
   All the Vestal Virgins' care ;
And the oldest altar shows
   But an older darkness there.
Age-encamped Oblivion
Tenteth every light that shone.

Yet shall we, for Suns that die,
   Wall our wanderings from desire ?
Or, because the Moon is high,
   Scorn to use a nearer fire ?
Lest some envious Pharaoh stir,
Make our lives our sepulchre ?

Nay !   Though Time with petty Fate
   Prison us and Emperors,
By our Arts do we create
   That which Time himself devours—
Such machines as well may run—
'Gainst the Horses of the Sun.

When we would a new abode,
   Space, our tyrant King no more,
Lays the long lance of the road
   At our feet and flees before,
Breathless, ere we overwhelm,
To submit a further realm !

BUDDHA AT KAMAKURA

1892

" And there is a Japanese idol at Kamakura."

O YE who tread the Narrow Way
By Tophet-flare to Judgment Day,
Be gentle when " the heathen " pray
  To Buddha at Kamakura !

To Him the Way, the Law, apart,
Whom Maya held beneath her heart,
Ananda's Lord, the Bodhisat,
  The Buddha of Kamakura.

For though He neither burns nor sees,
Nor hears ye thank your Deities,
Ye have not sinned with such as these,
  His children at Kamakura.

Yet spare us still the Western joke
When joss-sticks turn to scented smoke
The little sins of little folk
  That worship at Kamakura—

The grey-robed, gay-sashed butterflies
That flit beneath the Master's eyes.
He is beyond the Mysteries
  But loves them at Kamakura.

And whoso will, from Pride released,
Contemning neither creed nor priest,
May feel the Soul of all the East
    About him at Kamakura.

Yea, every tale Ananda heard,
Of birth as fish or beast or bird,
While yet in lives the Master stirred,
    The warm wind brings Kamakura.

Till drowsy eyelids seem to see
A-flower 'neath her golden *htee*
The Shwe-Dagon flare easterly
    From Burmah to Kamakura,

And down the loaded air there comes
The thunder of Thibetan drums,
And droned—" *Om mane padme hum's* "[1]—
    A world's-width from Kamakura.

Yet Brahmans rule Benares still,
Buddh-Gaya's ruins pit the hill,
And beef-fed zealots threaten ill
    To Buddha and Kamakura.

A tourist-show, a legend told,
A rusting bulk of bronze and gold,
So much, and scarce so much, ye hold
    The meaning of Kamakura?

[1] The Buddhist invocation.

But when the morning prayer is prayed,
Think, ere ye pass to strife and trade,
Is God in human image made
    No nearer than Kamakura ?

A SONG TO MITHRAS

(Hymn of the XXX Legion : circa A.D. 350)

MITHRAS, God of the Morning, our trumpets
    waken the Wall !
" Rome is above the Nations, but Thou art over
    all ! "
Now as the names are answered, and the guards
    are marched away,
Mithras, also a soldier, give us strength for the
    day !

Mithras, God of the Noontide, the heather swims
    in the heat.
Our helmets scorch our foreheads, our sandals
    burn our feet.
Now in the ungirt hour—now lest we blink and
    drowse,
Mithras, also a soldier, keep us true to our vows !

Mithras, God of the Sunset, low on the Western
    main—
Thou descending immortal, immortal to rise again !

Now when the watch is ended, now when the wine
    is drawn,
Mithras, also a soldier, keep us pure till the dawn !

Mithras, God of the Midnight, here where the
    great Bull dies,
Look on thy children in darkness. Oh take our
    sacrifice !
Many roads thou hast fashioned—all of them lead
    to the Light !
Mithras, also a soldier, teach us to die aright !

WHEN EARTH'S LAST PICTURE IS PAINTED

1892

When Earth's last picture is painted and the tubes
    are twisted and dried,
When the oldest colours have faded, and the
    youngest critic has died,
We shall rest, and, faith, we shall need it—lie down
    for an æon or two,
Till the Master of All Good Workmen shall put us
    to work anew.

And those that were good shall be happy ; they
    shall sit in a golden chair :
They shall splash at a ten-league canvas with
    brushes of comets' hair.

They shall find real saints to draw from—Mag-
    dalene, Peter, and Paul ;
They shall work for an age at a sitting and never
    be tired at all !

And only The Master shall praise us, and only
    The Master shall blame ;
And no one shall work for money, and no one
    shall work for fame,
But each for the joy of the working, and each, in
    his separate star,
Shall draw the Thing as he sees It for the God of
    Things as They are !

EDDI'S SERVICE

(A. D. 6 8 7)

EDDI, priest of St. Wilfrid
    In his chapel at Manhood End,
Ordered a midnight service
    For such as cared to attend.

But the Saxons were keeping Christmas,
    And the night was stormy as well.
Nobody came to service,
    Though Eddi rang the bell.

" 'Wicked weather for walking,"
    Said Eddi of Manhood End.

" But I must go on with the service
   For such as care to attend."

The altar-lamps were lighted,—
   An old marsh-donkey came,
Bold as a guest invited,
   And stared at the guttering flame.

The storm beat on at the windows,
   The water splashed on the floor,
And a wet, yoke-weary bullock
   Pushed in through the open door.

" How do I know what is greatest,
   How do I know what is least ?
That is My Father's business,"
   Said Eddi, Wilfrid's priest.

" But—three are gathered together—
   Listen to me and attend.
I bring good news, my brethren ! "
   Said Eddi of Manhood End.

And he told the Ox of a Manger
   And a Stall in Bethlehem,
And he spoke to the Ass of a Rider
   That rode to Jerusalem.

They steamed and dripped in the chancel,
   They listened and never stirred,
While, just as though they were Bishops,
   Eddi preached them The Word,

Till the gale blew off on the marshes
   And the windows showed the day,
And the Ox and the Ass together
   Wheeled and clattered away.

And when the Saxons mocked him,
   Said Eddi of Manhood End,
" I dare not shut His chapel
   On such as care to attend."

THE CHILDREN'S SONG

LAND of our Birth, we pledge to thee
Our love and toil in the years to be ;
When we are grown and take our place,
As men and women with our race.

Father in Heaven who lovest all,
Oh help Thy children when they call ;
That they may build from age to age,
An undefiled heritage.

Teach us to bear the yoke in youth,
With steadfastness and careful truth ;
That, in our time, Thy Grace may give
The Truth whereby the Nations live.

Teach us to rule ourselves alway,
Controlled and cleanly night and day ;

That we may bring, if need arise,
No maimed or worthless sacrifice.

Teach us to look in all our ends,
On Thee for judge, and not our friends ;
That we, with Thee, may walk uncowed
By fear or favour of the crowd.

Teach us the Strength that cannot seek,
By deed or thought, to hurt the weak ;
That, under Thee, we may possess
Man's strength to comfort man's distress.

Teach us Delight in simple things,
And Mirth that has no bitter springs ;
Forgiveness free of evil done,
And Love to all men 'neath the sun !

Land of our Birth, our faith, our pride,
For whose dear sake our fathers died ;
Oh Motherland, we pledge to thee,
Head, heart, and hand through the years to be !

CHARTRES WINDOWS
·
1925

COLOUR fulfils where Music has no power :
  By each man's light the unjudging glass betrays
All men's surrender, each man's holiest hour
  And all the lit confusion of our days—
Purfled with iron, traced in dusk and fire,
  Challenging ordered Time who, at the last,
  Shall bring it, grozed and leaded and wedged fast,
  To the cold stone that curbs or crowns desire.
Yet on the pavement that all feet have trod—
  Even as the Spirit, in her deeps and heights,
Turns only, and that voiceless, to her God—
  There falls no tincture from those anguished lights.
And Heaven's one light, behind them, striking through
Blazons what each man dreamed no other knew.

THE FAIRIES' SIEGE

I HAVE been given my charge to keep—
Well have I kept the same !
Playing with strife for the most of my life,
But this is a different game.

I'll not fight against swords unseen,
Or spears that I cannot view—
Hand him the keys of the place on your knees—
'Tis the Dreamer whose dreams come true !

Ask him his terms and accept them at once.
Quick, ere we anger him, go !
Never before have I flinched from the guns,
But this is a different show.
I'll not fight with the Herald of God
(I know what his Master can do !)
Open the gate, he must enter in state,
'Tis the Dreamer whose dreams come true !

I'd not give way for an Emperor,
I'd hold my road for a King—
To the Triple Crown I would not bow down—
But this is a different thing.
I'll not fight with the Powers of Air,
Sentry, pass him through !
Drawbridge let fall, 'tis the Lord of us all,
The Dreamer whose dreams come true !

THE HOUR OF THE ANGEL

SOONER or late—in earnest or in jest—
   (But the stakes are no jest) Ithuriel's Hour
Will spring on us, for the first time, the test
   Of our sole unbacked competence and power
   Up to the limit of our years and dower

Of judgment—or beyond.   But here we have
Prepared long since our garland or our grave.
　　For, at that hour, the sum of all our past,
　　Act, habit, thought, and passion, shall be cast
　　In one addition, be it more or less,
　　And as that reading runs so shall we do ;
　　Meeting, astounded, victory at the last,
　　Or, first and last, our own unworthiness.
And none can change us though they die to save !

THE PRAYER

　　My BROTHER kneels, so saith Kabir,
　　To stone and brass in heathen-wise,
　　But in my brother's voice I hear
　　My own unanswered agonies.
　　His God is as his fates assign,
　　His prayer is all the world's—and mine.